Tales of Four Lakes

Leech Lake, Gull Lake, Mille Lacs Lake, the Red Lakes & the Crow Wing River

by Duane R. Lund, Ph. D.

TABLE OF CONTENTS

6th Printing, 2002
5th Printing, 1994
4th Printing, 1989
3rd Printing, 1985
2nd Printing, 1979

Copyright © 1977 by
Dr. Duane R. Lund
Staples, Miinnesota 56479

Printed in the United States of America
By:
Nordell Graphic Communications
Staples, Minnesota 56479

PREFACE

Tales of Four Lakes and a River is a special look at Minnesota history. Lakes and streams have been entwined in the development of our state and our way of life from the beginning. Leech, Gull, Mille Lacs, and the Red Lakes, as well as the Crow Wing River, have exciting histories of their own, but to learn about them collectively, is to learn about Minnesota.

Their waters have reflected Indian civilizations, explorers' canoes, the packs of the fur traders, the crosses and cloaks of missionaries, the pikes of the loggers, the giant wheels of ox carts, the nets of commercial fishermen, the homes and farms of early settlers, and today's countless contrivances of recreation. And they are very much a part of the high quality of living of which our state can rightfully boast.

But why these four lakes and why this river? Because they are among the largest, because they are among the most historic, because they represent well the thousands of other lakes and streams of our state, because they are today among the most beautiful and most significant, and because they are among the best known to and most deeply loved by the author.

DEDICATION

To Elmer L. Andersen

former -

Legislator
Governor of Minnesota
President, Minnesota Historical Society
Chairman, University of Minnesota Board of Regents
District Governor, Rotary International

Industrial Leader, Environmentalist, Humanitarian

He has never grown weary of well doing; he is Mr. Minnesota.

CHAPTER ONE
A Common Prologue

Who was the first to dip his paddle into the clear waters of the Crow Wing River?

Who was the first to look out across the vast expanse of the Red Lakes, trying to see land and wondering whether he had found an inland sea or even an ocean?

Who first harvested the wild rice on Leech Lake? What mother worked it into food for her family?

Who first picked blueberries on the shores of Gull Lake - probably swatting mosquitoes and deerflies between handfuls?

Who caught and enjoyed the first walleye pike out of Mille Lacs? Was he an angler? Did he use a net? Or was it a spear?

We will never know. These early adventurers shall remain forever nameless and faceless. But they were real people and they were here! And we can speculate about them. They were in all probability of the Indian race. We can be quite certain they were all born on the North American continent. In all likelihood their ancestors crossed the Bering Straits from Asia a good many generations earlier, but we have no way of knowing how soon they worked their way *east* after arriving on this continent. The current theory is that the prehistoric people went south along the west coast and then worked *north* to this area in mid continent. (The white explorers, in contrast, came from the opposite coast) And all of these events took place several thousands of years before Christ walked our earth.

White man is really a "Johnny Come Lately" on the Minnesota scene. Even the earliest of the great white explorers did not reach our state until well into the 17th century.[1] Radisson and Groseilliers may have been here in the 1650's. The Sieur du Lhut (Daniel Greysolon), for whom the City of Duluth has been named, was definitely here in 1679. It was the next year that the Franciscan Friar, Father Louis Hennepin, arrived as a member of an exploration party commissioned by La Salle to find the source of the Mississippi River - which had been discovered only seven years earlier by Marquette and Jolliet. It was 1688 when twenty-year old Jacques de Noyon reached Rainy Lake and that year or shortly thereafter followed Rainy River to the Lake of the Woods. Le Sueur arrived here just before the turn of the century. It was in 1766 that Jonathan Carver, the English explorer, worked his way up the Mississippi and wintered with the Sioux on the Minnesota River. The Pike and Cass Expeditions explored the Mississippi in 1805 and 1820 respectively. By the white man's calendar, Minnesota is really quite new country. It is possible that the span of time represented by white man's association with Minnesota is less than five percent of human history in the area!

If Indians were the first inhabitants of Minnesota and the first to depend on our state's lakes and rivers for transportation and food - then, which Indians? Which tribes were here first? We really don't know. By the time the earliest white traders, trappers, explorers and missionaries reached this area, the Sioux and Algonquins (more

[1] This statement stands until there is better evidence of visits by Vikings or others.

specifically the Dakotas and Ojibways) occupied our state. The Ojibway were barely here ahead of Du Luth; they were just then working into the state from the north and east because of pressures from the well-armed Iroquois tribes along the eastern seaboard. The Dakotas and other Sioux tribes, on the other hand, were firmly in control of nearly all the area we now call Minnesota. They had been in the southern part of the state since 1,000 A.D. or earlier but had taken over most of the northern portions less than a century before.

Archeologists have given us many clues about earlier tribes. When man first came to this area, perhaps at the end of the fourth glacial period, he found larger lakes than we have today - and perhaps more of them. Lake Agassiz covered most of northwestern Minnesota and portions of the Dakotas, Manitoba and Ontario. It was larger than all of the Great Lakes put together! The present shorelines of our major lakes were probably established between 2,000 B.C. and the time of Christ.

Most clues to early Indian civilizations may be found in their burial mounds where weapons, tools, pottery, pipes, and ornaments were laid to rest along with the dead. The most ancient of these mounds in Minnesota contain ivory artifacts, indicating that these people were contemporary with the wooly mammoth. Later mounds[1] contain copper tools and gaffs which have been dated at about 2,000 B.C. making them possibly the earliest metal items fabricated by man on either North or South America. Some mounds, however, were not burial places but are the remains of dwelling places made of earth. Before the coming of gunpowder, earthen dwellings were fairly secure and there is some evidence they were used more frequently than bark wigwams or lodges. Because they take longer to build and certainly were not portable, their use would indicate these people did not move as often. The Indians of the plains have long used earth-homes and many examples can be found to this day.

Sometime before the birth of Christ, a people moved into the Minnesota-Ontario area whom we have named "the Laurel Culture." Their burial mounds were huge. The largest was forty-feet high and more than 100 feet long. Some of the skeletal remains from the Laurel period were of a race larger and heavier than modern-day Indian. The bones were buried in bundles, indicating that the bodies had originally been placed on scaffolds or in shallow graves and allowed to decompose. To add to the mystery - shell ornaments were found which have been determined to have come from either the Gulf of Mexico or the Pacific Ocean.

Many archeologists believe that the earliest mound builders in our state were the Hopewell Indians of southern Minnesota. Northern tribes may have learned from them. Changes in pottery is another example of the influence of southern cultures on the north. Early samples of pottery in the woodlands area were tall and elongated. Later, they apparently copied the round or global effect of the pottery of the Indians of southern Minnesota.

It is probable that the bow and arrow were unknown to Minnesota until the coming of the Laurel people.

Some time around 1,000 A.D. a new people arrived in northern Minnesota and established what we have labeled as the "Blackduck Culture."[2] Whether they pushed the Laurel people out or assimilated them is not known, perhaps some of each. The Blackduck people buried their dead in pits, and then built mounds over the remains. Two such burial mounds, dated around 1,200 A.D. and located at the mouth of the

[1]Found in the Rainy Lake area.
[2]Both the Blackduck and the Laurel people are sometimes referred to as "The Woodland Culture."

Rainy River, contained a spectacular find: seven skulls - modeled and decorated with paint, as well as a variety of ornaments, pipes, shells, antlers, etc.

The Blackduck culture prevailed until the 17th century in the woodlands of Minnesota.

Also around 1,000 A.D., another Indian civilization, known as the "Mississippi Culture," moved into southern Minnesota from the south and southwest. Among them were tribes of the Sioux Nation. It is possible, however, that other Sioux tribes were already here.

The Indians of the Mississippi knew something about agriculture and were particularly dependent on maize (Indian corn). Because maize did not grow well in the colder climate of northern Minnesota, the Mississippi Culture did not move north of an imaginary line between the present site of Minnesota's Twin Cities and Lake Traverse (until the 17th century). During the 1600's, the Sioux came to dominate all but the extreme far north of the Minnesota region. However, during the latter half of the 17th century, the Ojibway began their migration from the east into our state.

Included sometime in the pre-Dakota era was a tribe called "Gros Ventre"[1] by the French. They were a remarkable people. Eventually pushed west into the Dakotas, they established their earthen dwellings in villages on the banks of the Missouri River near the Mandans. The tribes grew quite similar over the years. The Mandans probably also came by way of Minnesota and some anthropologists feel the two tribes are related. Both peoples placed a high priority on cleanliness and were known to bathe twice a day, using a white clay as a cleansing agent. Ojibway visitors to the Gros Ventres in the 1800's were impressed with their knowledge of the Minnesota lakes region and were shown a map of sorts on birch bark which included Sandy Lake. Nearly wiped out by smallpox and war parties, other tribes developed a sympathy for them and eventually offered them protection.[2]

But the Dakotas and a few Ojibway were the tribes which were living on the banks of Minnesota's lakes and streams when white men first arrived on the scene in the 1600's. These were the people with whom the trappers, traders, explorers, missionaries, and developers had to deal in the settling of our state. As we have said, the Sioux were here first. The Ojibway moved in from the east and slowly but surely pressured the Sioux out of their woodland villages into southern Minnesota and on to the plains of the Dakotas. White men "finished the job" by driving the Sioux from southern Minnesota in 1863 - following the Sioux uprisings which began in the Mankato-New Ulm area the previous year. The Ojibway are still here and some Sioux have returned.

The Dakotas and the Ojibway were of different origin. They came from different ancestral stock with different languages, different customs and different traditions. At the time of the settling of the Atlantic shores of North America by the Europeans, the eastern half of what is now Canada and the United States was inhabited by three distinctly different groups of Indians: The Algonquin, the Sioux,. and the Iroquois.

[1]The Ojibway called them "The ancient people."
[2]Warren, William, History of the Ojibways, Minnesota Historical Collection, Volume 5.

Prehistoric Mound, at Mound Park, Laurel, Minn. Height: 28 ft. Width: 115 ft. One of the largest found in Minnesota.

Their languages, for example, were so entirely different they could communicate only by signs. Within each of these cultures were numerous related tribes:

SIOUX	ALGONQUIN	IROQUOIS
Dakota (with seven councils)	Ojibway[1] (Chippewa)	Mohawk
Sisseton	Ottawa	Oneida
Teton	Sac	Onondaga
Yankton	Fox	Cayuga
Yanktonai	Potawatomi	Seneca
Wahpeton	Illinois	
Wahpakute	Shawnee	(these five had a close alliance)
Mdewakanton	Miami	
Iowa	Kickapoo	Tuscarora
Oto	Menominees	Erie
Missouri	Cree	Hurons
Omaha		
Osage		
Ponca		
Hidatsa		
Crow		
Mandan		
Assiniboin		
Winnebago		

In the 17th century, as the colonies were being established, the Iroquois inhabited the coastal area west to the Appalachians; the Sioux occupied the western part of the midwest, with some tribes found farther to the south and southwest; and the Algonquins were generally in between with a few tribes as far east as New England.[2] The individual sub-tribes were spread out within these general regions. The five tribes of the Iroquois Lodge (Oneida, Mohawk, Onondaga, Cayuga, and Seneca) were in and around what is now New York State. The Eries were along the coast; the Tuscarora to the south. The Hurons had their troubles with their Iroquois cousins and moved north. The hostility grew and a "Neutral Nation" was allowed to exist in between them as a buffer.

Among the tribes of the Sioux Nation, the Dakotas occupied present day Minnesota wit the Assiniboins[3] to the far north, the Winnebago to the east (Wisconsin), the Hidatsa, Crow, and Mandans to the west (Dakotas), and the others to the south (Oto, Ponca, Osage, Omaha, Iowa, and the Missouris).

The Algonquin were generally scattered throughout the area between the Sioux and the Iroquois. The Ojibway were by far the largest of the Algonquin tribes. For an

[1]There are several acceptable spellings of "Ojibway", including "Objiwa" (Schoolcraft's spelling) and "Ojibwey." The tribe was also called "Chippewa" perhaps a French corruption of "Ojibway." "Chippewa" often appears on treaties and other legal documents. Theories of the origin and meaning of the word include "to pucker" which could apply to the design of their moccasins or to the effect on the skins of their victims placed too close to the fire. They have sometimes called themselves "Anishinanbay."

[2]Ojibway tradition tells of when these people once lived by the Atlantic.

[3]The Assiniboins once lived in Wisconsin. They had a problem with their Sioux cousins (The Winnebagos) and were driven out of the area. They fled to the far north along the Minnesota-Ontario border and placed themselves at the mercy of the Cree. Anxious for allies against the Dakotas, the Cree took them in and together they formed a strong and lasting alliance. "Assiniboin" may be loosely translated as "Sioux who live in the rocky region."

unknown length of time they were involved in "The Three Fires Confederacy" with the Ottawa and the Potawatomi. They separated, according to Ojibway tradition, about 400 years ago. The Ojibway covered an area so vast (particularly after they fled from the Iroquois) that they were sometimes described as four separate groups:
(1) Southeastern Ojibway or "Bungi" - between Lake Michigan & Lake Erie.
(2) Southwestern Ojibway - Wisconsin, the Michigan Peninsula and later - southern Minnesota.
(3) Northern Ojibway or Salteaux - Ontario and eventually northern Minnesota.
(4) Plains Ojibway - Manitoba and northern North Dakota.

Although there was, no doubt, a good deal of strife over the centuries between the various tribes and sub-tribes, the first extensive (recorded) warfare was in the late 1640's. Prior to that time the Indians did not have gunpowder and there seemed to be enough land with good hunting, fishing, and trapping for all. Early explorers reported considerable fighting but it was usually on a small scale and usually seasonal. During the months of good hunting and harvesting there was little time for fighting. Winter made warfare most uncomfortable and the snow made tracking much too easy to carry out revenge. Then, too, cold and famine were the greater enemies that time of year. Yet, fighting and scalp-taking were very much a way of life. A good deal of bloodshed took place over hunting grounds, wild rice beds, and even over misunderstandings growing out of inter-tribal marriages and family spats. But most fighting was localized and between neighboring tribes.
    As the colonists traded their guns and powder to the Indians, the stage was being set for inter-tribal warfare far more devastating. We have already told how the Hurons split off from the Iroquois Lodge and moved farther north. The day finally came when the "Neutral Nation" in between was not a sufficient buffer to prevent the well-armed Iroquis from launching an all out attack to rid themselves once and for all of their enemies. The five Iroquois allies, armed with weapons provided by the English, Dutch, and Swedish colonists, set out to annihilate the Hurons and anyone else suspected of aligning themselves with them - including the Eries, the Neutral Nation, the eastern Algonquins, and any Frenchmen who happened to become involved. Thousands[1] were scalped and mutilated. The survivors retreated where they could - west, and thus began the migration of the Ojibway towards their future home - Minnesota.
    The first direct contact between the Whites and the Ojibway was probably in 1612. As explorers, accompanied by their priests, ventured westward they found the Ojibway scattered over a large area, both north and south of Lake Superior. When missionaries arrived at Sault Ste. Marie in 1640, they found a sizable concentration of Ojibway. This village grew to an estimated population of 2000 by 1680 - a virtual metropolis by the standards of the northern tribes. After 1680 the Ojibway moved farther west and the village declined in both size and importance. A new concentration developed at La Pointe[2] - on Madeline Island at the mouth of Chequamegon Bay on Lake Superior. This new capital of the Ojibway Nation eventually had a population of about 1,000.

[1]Estimates of deaths ran as high as 10,000.
[2]LaPointe was occupied by the Hurons and the Ottawas for about twenty years prior to the take over by the Ojibway.

The Ojibway migration routes lead both north and south of Lake Superior; the majority chose the southern route and settled in Wisconsin. Those using the northern way settled along the north shore of Lake Superior and around Rainy Lake and Lake of the Woods. Contrary to what we might expect, there was little confrontation at first between the Ojibway and the Sioux, even though they were traditional enemies. The basic reason was economic. The French needed the furs of the Minnesota Lake region and knew virtually none would be available if the Sioux and Ojibway were at war. The Sioux and the Ojibway realized too that there would be no trade items available to them if they had to spend their time defending themselves against an enemy instead of collecting furs. Du Luth was the chief negotiator and genuine hero of the peace-keeping effort. He wintered with the Ojibway at Sault Ste. Marie in 1678-79 and during that time developed a good working relationship with both the French traders and the Indians. With the coming of the ice break-up in the spring, Du Luth lead a band of Ojibway to a site near the city which now bears his name, and there held a council with several tribes in an attempt to expand the fur trade industry into Minnesota and southern Ontario. At this meeting, representatives of the Dakota, Cree, and Assiniboin pledged friendship and cooperation with the French and Ojibway. No mean accomplishment! Du Luth also used the occasion to lay claim to the entire upper Mississippi area for France. In the same year (1679), Du Luth founded a trading post at Grand Portage on Lake Superior. From this base he established trade with the Sioux tribes of the lake region with the Ojibway as the middlemen! Grand Portage was destined to become the rendezvous point for the voyageurs from Montreal ("porkeaters") and those from Lake Ahabasca and other western points ("men of the north"). Because it was impossible to travel all the way from Montreal to the trading posts in the west and return in a single season, a meeting place was necessary for the exchange of furs and trade goods. Grand Portage was that place.

Trade developed rapidly. LaSalle reported in 1682 that the Ojibway were trading with the Dakotas as far as 150 miles to the west. The peaceful arrangement allowed large numbers of Ojibway to settle in Wisconsin and along both the north and south shores of Lake Superior. But the peace was too good to last. With a history of tribal conflicts, fears and suspicions were latent in everyone's minds. Small incidents were quickly magnified. Any death called for revenge. By 1730 the truce was an uneasy one.

It was this testy atmosphere that greeted the French-Canadian explorer, Pierre La Verendrye, upon his arrival at Lake of the Woods in 1732. His construction of Fort St. Charles on the Northwest Angle of that lake helped keep the peace for a time, but the warpath which lead from the plains of the Dakotas to its terminal point at present day Warroad, on Lake of the Woods, was once again in use. La Verendrye, like other Frenchmen, allied himself with the Ojibway. It is not surprising, therefore, that the Sioux eventually launched a direct attack on the French. The Dakota massacre on Lake of the Woods of twenty-one Frenchmen - including La Verendrye's eldest son, Jean Baptiste, and his priest, Father Alneau - really marked the beginning of all-out war between the Dakotas and the Ojibways and their friends the Crees and the Assiniboins. In the same year (1736) the Ojibway gained a measure of revenge for La Verendrye by launching a raiding party from La Pointe into southeastern Minnesota. The Ojibway had begged La Verendrye to lead an attack against the Sioux, but in his wisdom he refused. He knew that open warfare would bring more Sioux to that area and could very well mean the end for sometime to the fur trade business. His entire expedition was financed by Montreal merchants who had been growing more and more demanding for a better return on their investment. Without furs there would be no support from the East.

In spite of the efforts of La Vérendrye and other Frenchmen,[1] warfare continued between the Ojibway and the Dakotas in a state of almost continuous escalation until 1770. But now we are getting ahead of our story because much of the early history of our "Four Lakes and a River" will deal specifically with the open warfare which broke out at this time between the Dakotas and the Ojibways and their allies.

It was during this time, however, that La Pointe reached its zenith of importance. Not only did it become a center for trade, but it was also one of the major bases from which the Ojibway would launch their attacks on the Sioux. La Pointe remained the Ojibway capital until about 1770. By that time the French and their Indian allies had lost the "French and Indian War" to the British. The treaty signed in Paris in 1763 gave this part of North America to the English, and by 1770 many of the French traders had moved out of the area. Also by 1770 the Ojibway had won some key battles involving small armies of warriors and had effectively driven the Dakotas from their villages throughout the entire lake region. Minnesota was therefore starting to open up for settlement by the victors and so the residents of La Pointe moved west.

William Warren,[2] the celebrated Ojibway author and Territorial legislator, tells of another reason the tribe left La Pointe. He calls it "the darkest hour of Ojibway history." In the last years at La Pointe, the people were intimidated by santanic medicine men who promoted cannibalism. The newly dead were unearthed at night, roasted, and eaten. Anyone refusing to participate could very well become the next victim. According to Warren's research, the Ojibway finally concluded the only answer was to flee. Not a pleasant story, but all civilizations and all races have pages in their histories they would prefer to tear out, throw away, and forget.[3] Warren also tells of a far happier day at La Pointe which gives us an excellent picture of Ojibway life of that day. He wrote that the practice of farming reached its peak for the Ojibway during their stay at La Pointe. He described the gardens as "extensive" and said that "they raised large quantities of Num-dem-in (Indian corn) and pumpkins." He described the mainland as "overrun with moose, bear, elk, and deer." Warren wrote thus concerning the early days at La Pointe - before guns and powder were common:

"Every stream which emptied into the lake, abounded in beaver, otter, and muskrat, and the fish which swam in its clear water could not be surpassed in quality or quantity in any other spot on earth. They manufactured their nets of the inner bark of the bass and cedar trees, and from the fibres of the nettle. They made thin knives from the rib of bones of the moose and buffalo. And a stone tied to the end of a stick, with which they broke branches and sticks, answered them the purpose of an axe. From the thighbone of a muskrat they ground their awls, and fire was obtained by the friction of two dry sticks. Bows of hard wood, or bone, sharp stone-headed arrows, and spear points made also of bone, formed their implements of war and hunting. With ingeniously made traps and dead-falls, they caught the wily beaver, whose flesh was

---

[1]Some historians believe that the French felt that there would be no permanent peace without the destruction of the Sioux and that the best way to accomplish this was to arm the Ojibway and let them do the fighting. There may have been some truth to this theory but it is not substantiated by the journals of such French leaders as La Vérendrye.

[2]Warren, William W., History of the Ojibways, Minnesota Historical Colleciton, Volume 5.

[3]There is also a legend of a brief period of cannibalism on Cross Lake; there may have been some connection.

their most dainty food, and whose skins made them warm blankets. To catch the moose and larger animals, they built long and gradually narrowing inclosures of branches, wherein they would first drive and then kill them, one after another, with their barbed arrows. They also caught them in nooses made of tough hide and hung from a strong bent treee, over the road that these animals commonly travelled to feed, or find water. Bear they caught in dead-falls, which were so unfailing that they have retained their use to this day . . ."

Before turning to the individual histories of our "Four Lakes and a River," it makes sense that we take a closer look at the Dakota and Ojibway peoples. After all, they enjoyed these waters long before the white man arrived on the scene and, as we have said, these were the people with whom the white settlers had to deal.

First, let us generalize that the people of these two great tribes were far more alike then they were different. Both, while in Minnesota, were dependent upon the woods, lakes, prairies, and streams for survival. The trees, especially the birch, furnished materials for both shelter and transportation. Animal life provided meat and clothing. Bones were used for tools and hooks. Fish and fowl made for the finest of eating. The berries and nuts of the woods and the wild rice of the lakes and streams were also important foods. Stones were shaped into both tools and weapons. Before the coming of guns and powder, both peoples used spears and bow and arrows. Clay soil was used to fashion pottery and utensils. With the coming of the trader, all sorts of ironware, knives and trinkets became available. Metal soon replaced stone as arrowheads and was also used in other weapons. Indians took well to gardening. Pierre La Verendrye taught them how on Lake of the Woods in the 1730's and Simon Dawson was astounded to find an eight acre garden on an island in the Northwest Angle of the Lake of the Woods in 1857. The Sioux apparently learned gardening on their own or from other tribes. Most of what the Indian took from his environment was for survival, but he did harvest one luxury - tobacco. In Minnesota, the chief ingredient came from the dried inner bark of the kinnikinic (red willow) which was often mixed with powdered leaves and roots from other plants. Pipes made from stone (catlinite)[1] taken from the quarries near Pipestone, Minnesota, were used by many tribes - often long distances from this source. Smoking also marked ceremonial occasions, much as toasting with alcoholic drinks has been customary for centuries on special occasions in other civilizations.

Both tribes loved paint and feathers. Both were a singing and dancing people. They were gregarious and lovers of feasts and games. The Sioux particularly enjoyed "betting."

There were few differences in how the Sioux and Ojibway made use of nature's bounty while residing in our state. Both, for example, harvested the sap from the maple tree and used it to make sugar. In late March or early April, the return of the first crow caused great rejoicing because it signaled the coming of spring and the rising of the sap in the maple trees. Winter hunting encampments would break up. The families, relations and even whole villages would move to their traditional "sugar bush" area where they would stay until May. Permanent lodges were located at these sites. They were large, usually measuring from 10 to 20 feet wide and 25 to 40 feet long. Sometimes smaller, temporary huts were built - called "wig-wa-si-ga-mig" by the Ojibway. Whites nicknamed them "wigwams." The trees were tapped by cutting a

[1]Named for George Catlin, an artist and explorer who claimed to be the discoverer of the pipestone quarries. Others were actually there before him but he originally received the credit.

slash and driving a cedar splinter or carved spigot into the wood. The sap dripped off the splinter and was then collected in containers on the ground (made from birchbark). Syrup was made by boiling the sap for days over an open fire. Although the syrup was sometimes used for food, it was usually thickened by continued boiling and then when it was the right consistency, placed in a basswood trough where it was gently stirred until it became granulated, thus forming sugar.

Often times the syrup was poured into molds and allowed to harden. This "hard sugar" could be stored more conveniently for use throughout the year. One family could prepare as much as 500 pounds of maple sugar in a single season. The hard sugar was eaten as a food or confection; granulated sugar was used as a seasoning or flavoring agent; and a beverage was made by dissolving the maple sugar in water.

Spring was also the time for fishing, trapping, and hunting. In addition to using nets and traps, spawning fish were often speared at night with a birch bark or pine knot torch for light. Migratory waterfowl were again found on the Indian menu. Muskrats were easier to trap. All in all, spring was a time for both work and rejoicing. Celebrations, feasting and religious ceremonies accompanied the spring activities.

Syrup was made by boiling sap for days over an open fire. Courtesy of the Minnesota Historical Society

July and August were a season for berry picking. The braves may have been helpful in locating the berry patches, but the women and children did the picking. Just as today, the woodlands had an abundance of blueberries, chokecherries, pincherries, raspberries, strawberries, and cranberries (both low and high bush). Every effort was made to preserve the fruit for use later in the year. Some berries were dried whole; others were dried and then pulverized. Boiling was sometimes used, particularly with raspberries. It was also at this time that ducks and geese became quite helpless during a period of moulting and young birds were taken just before they were large enough to fly. Unsportsmanlike? Not when you're talking about food for survival!

September brought the wild rice harvest and another occasion to feast and celebrate. It was perhaps even a greater time for reunions and socializing than the sugar camps. Most harvesting was done by the women, usually two to a canoe. While one paddled or poled the boat through the rice bed, the other sat in front and pulled the rice over the canoe, beating the heads with a stick - thus dislodging the mature kernels. Since all of the rice in each head did not mature at the same time, the harvesters could cover the same area several times a few days apart.[1]

The kernels were further separated from the husks by beating or trampling and then the chaff was blown away by throwing the rice into the air on a windy day. The kernels were then parched by the fire.

The same animals that are found in Minnesota today were here centuries ago - plus a few more. The earliest inhabitants of our state found such huge beasts as the wooly mammoth and the giant bison. Buffalo, caribou, and elk were common in Minnesota - even after white men first arrived. Most animals, such as moose, were probably more plentiful than today, but others, such as deer, may have been less plentiful. But for all of the animal life, hunting was not always easy. Such primitive weapons as spears and bows and arrows gave wild game a great advantage. Predators and disease probably took a greater toll than the Indians, and severe winters were hard on both the hunter and the hunted.

Courtesy of the Minnesota Historical Society

Chippewa Scalp Dance—from watercolor by Peter Rindisbacker in West Point Museum. "White explorers were impressed with the muscular physique of Indians; early drawings made them look somewhat like Greek Athletes!"

Although there were few differences in how the Ojibway and the Dakotas made use of nature's bounty, in many ways the tribes were not alike. Language was perhaps the most significant difference. Even though the Algonquins and the Sioux had been neighbors for centuries, even the basic root words bore no resemblance. It is likely that the ancestors of these two tribes migrated to North America at different periods of history and from different parts of Asia. Differences in facial and other physical characteristics were accented by diverse clothing, head gear, and hair styles. Furthermore, the Sioux were of a tall but athletic build, while the Ojibway were more

[1]The University of Minnesota has developed strains of wild rice in which most of the kernels in each head mature about the same time without falling, thus making one-time harvesting possible in today's commercial paddies. Thus far, the quality of this "non-shattering" variety is not quite as good and more susceptible to disease. For this reason most commercial growers have returned to more natural strains. However the University of Minnesota feels at this time (1977) that they are very close to some significant breakthroughs.

stocky but sturdy. White explorers were impressed with the muscular physique of the Indians; early drawings made them look somewhat like Greek athletes!

Both tribes were very religious, but there were significant differences as well as similarities.

Both believed in a Supreme Being or Great Spirit. Both believed in a life after death (happy hunting ground). Both had a multitude of lesser gods or spirits - usually taken from nature. The Sioux labeled the spirits or the unknown as "waken;" the Ojibway called them "manitou;" Religion called for such virtues as patience, truth, and honesty, but curses were called down upon enemies. Superstitions and religious legends were numerous and varied somewhat from tribe to tribe and village to village. Gods were worshipped in prayers, offerings, chants and dances. The Ojibway, in particular, were conscientious about offering prayers whenever food was harvested or taken in a hunt. Visions and dreams were generated by fasting and meditation.

"The happy hunting ground" was a place where the Indian was free from his struggle for survival and all the necessities of life were easily attained. Chief Bemidji described the Indian's "Hell" as a place where the hungry Indian could see hundreds of walleyes through six feet of ice with no way to cut through, or a deer was always just going over the second hill as he came over the first, or he was very cold and all the wood was too wet to start a fire.

Medicine men were both priests and healers. When herbs or other medicines did not work they exorcised evil spirits. They practiced the "laying on of hands" to invoke a blessing.

The help of the gods was sought before each serious endeavor, whether it be waging war, hunting or whatever.

Dances often included a religious or other serious purpose and were not performed as mere entertainment.

The Ojibway had a religious-cultural hero named "Nanabozho," who created the world for the Indian and taught him about the Great Spirit and religious practices. These practices were called "Midewiwin," and they were characterized by secret ceremonies and initiations including a guardian spirit for each and a "totem" spirit for each family group or relation. The Ojibways had about twenty totems with as many as 1,000 members in a totem family. It was taboo for members of the same totem to marry. There were a few examples of the totem practice among Sioux tribes but it is believed that these can be traced in each case to intermarriages with the Ojibway. The totem was symbolized by a bird, animal, reptile, or fish. In addition, each Ojibway carried a medicine bag which contained herbs and items such as shells which represented special powers and protection. The priests were called "Mides."

Polygamy was permitted by both tribes with the male taking more than one wife.

Upon death, following a ceremony and appropriate mourning,[1] bodies were sometimes bundled on scaffolds or placed in trees - particularly during the cold time of the year - and buried later. The Ojibway traditionally buried their dead in a sitting position facing west. A long, low house-like shelter was constructed over the grave. Food was placed here along with all the deceased would need in the way of tools and weapons to help him in his journey westward "across the river" to his eternal reward. A carved or drawn symbol of the appropriate totem was often placed outside the shelter.

---

[1]Periods of mourning were often characterized by much crying and loud wailing.

Courtesy of the Minnesota Historical Society

Ojibway Mide Lodge—"Ojibway religious practices were called "Midewiwin, and they were characterized by secret ceremonies and initiations."

William Warren, the Ojibway author we have previously quoted, was a self-ordained Christian missionary. He told in his "History of the Ojibway" something about his efforts to convert his people to Christianity. He was surprised that the elders of the tribes often knew the Old Testament stories of the Bible - but identified the heroes with Indian names. This led him to speculate that the Indian people could have been descendents of the "Ten Lost Tribes of Israel!"

Missionaries had great difficulty in converting the Indian peoples. To this day many Indians have held to their traditional beliefs; others have adopted a curious blend of these beliefs and Christianity. However, many were "converted" and these converts often had greater success than the white missionaries in introducing the teachings of Jesus to the Indians. But generally there was great resistance and many missionaries dispaired at behavior "degrading and immoral" by their standards. Alcohol arrived almost as soon as the missionaries and made their task even more trying. The nomadic traits of the Indian tribes made it difficult to work with them long enough to have an impact. Father Alneau, the Lake of the Woods martyr, was among those directed to locate the Mandan tribe which supposedly stayed for generations in one place and "enjoyed" a more advanced civilization and standard of living.[1] He did not

[1]The Mandans are believed to have spent some time in Minnesota before settling in central North Dakota. Some who believe in the authenticity of the Kensington Runestone (not generally accepted by historians) attribute the higher standard of living to association with the Vikings described on the Runestone. They further support this theory by the fact the Mandans sometimes used moat-like waterways to protect their permanent dwellings. According to legend, a fair-skinned people lived among the Mandans prior to the smallpox epidemic of 1782. We are also told that a band of marauding Ojibways, Crees, and Assiniboins came upon a helpless tribe in the Mandan area - either Mandans or Gros Ventres - at the time of the epidemic and took an enormous scalp from a giant of a man as one of their trophies. Did the thick, bushy scalp belong to a descendant of the Vikings??? This scalp, along with the others taken is believed to have been a carrier of smallpox germs back into the lake region.

live long enough to find them, but his sponsors, the La Vérendryes, eventually explored the Dakotas.

The Roman Catholic Church and every major Protestant denomination sent missionaries to the Indians. Because the French came first to this area, the earliest missionaries were Catholic. They were followed by Episcopalians, Methodists, Presbyterians, and representatives of all other "mainline" churches as well as numerous smaller sects. In addition to spreading the gospel, these men of God deserve much credit for the journals they kept and for their contributions to map making and other results of exploration. They also showed the Indian people a better side of white civilization.

Courtesy of the Minnesota Historical Society

Ojibway grave houses. "Periods of mourning were often characterized by much crying and loud wailing."

To continue our comparison, the basic shelters of the two tribes also developed differently. The Sioux used earthen dwellings, particularly on the prairies, while the Ojibway used birchbark - covered lodges. While living in the wooded areas of Minnesota, the Sioux also used birchbark-covered dwellings, particularly when they were interested in portability. But hides were often substituted for birchbark, particularly during the colder months. The basic shapes of the shelters were also different; The Ojibway preferred a dome or rounded shape to their lodges while the Dakotas chose the pointed cone-shaped tepees. Both had openings in the roof for smoke to escape from an open fire.

Both used bichbark canoes, but when the Sioux tribes first arrived in Minnesota it is believed they used dugouts and boats made of skins stretched over wood frames.

As may be expected, other differences appeared as the Dakotas retreated westward to the prairies. The canoe was replaced by the horse. Diets changed when wild rice and certain berries were no longer available. Wood for fuel was sometimes replaced by "buffalo chips."[1] Traditionally, the Dakotas were more dependent on maize (Indian corn). No doubt this was because the Sioux tribes lived so long in warmer climates. As

[1]Dried manure.

the Dakotas left the woodland regions they became especially dependent on the buffalo for both the meat and the hide. In fact, the hide was a good trade item for the Dakotas before the white man sent his own hunters into the west. A favorite food of the Dakotas was called "pemican." It was made from dried and pounded buffalo meat and flavored with berries. This, too, became a trade item as the Whites of the early frontier cultivated a taste for it.

The Sioux were supposedly more warlike, but the Algonquin tribes could be just as ruthless when dealing with their enemies.

Writers have lead us to believe that other differences were perhaps the result of the earlier contacts of the Ojibway with the whites. As a result, they were supposedly not only better armed than the Dakotas but also had the benefit of such traded items as blankets, steel traps, iron kettles, and steel knives. In contrast, the Dakotas were pictured as just emerging from a stone age civilization.

Present day historians discount this theory and point out that the French had been trading with the Sioux since the 1600's.

In conclusion, we should point out that Minnesota was really rather sparsely settled inthe days of Du Luth and Father Hennepin. The Minnesota Indian population today is more than twenty thousand. It was very likely less than this in the 17th and 18th centuries.

Ojibway Lodge

Courtesy of the Minnesota Historical Society

Sioux Teepee

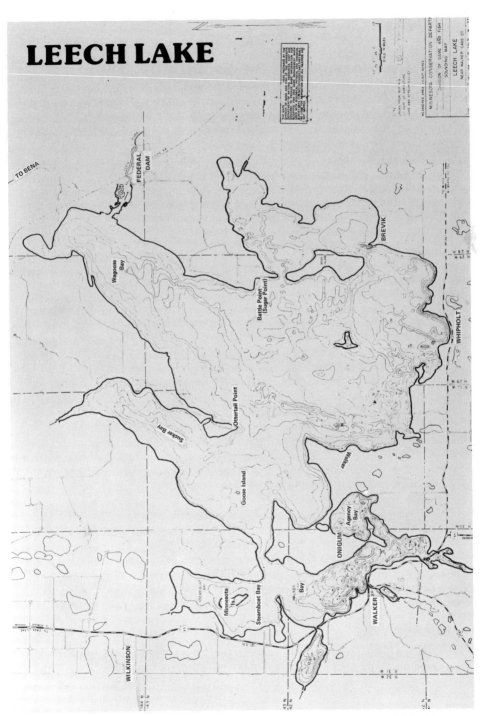

LEECH LAKE

Courtesy of the Minnesota Department of Natural Resources

CHAPTER TWO
Leech Lake

A LEGEND OF THE ORIGIN OF THE LAKE

Several generations ago when the Pillager band of Ojibway Indians inhabited Bear Island on Leech Lake and boasted that they were "the most ferocious of all the Chippewa tribes of northern Minnesota,"[1] the old men told this story to the children about the creation of Leech Lake:

More moons back than any Chippewa can remember, when all the Indian tribes were away except a squaw and her daughter, an evil spirit one day captured the maiden and carried her away to a great dry plain where he lived in a wigwam of solid rock. While pining for freedom she was visited by an emissary of the supreme deity of the Indians, who gave her a peculiar black stone and told her to make of it a spear and strike with it a certain spot on the rocks. She did as the spirit told her and at once a great spring of water welled out and flowed rapidly over the plain. It began to fill all the vast space, and as it rose, the maiden climbed higher and higher until she almost reached the top of the rock, when the water ceased rising. Meanwhile the evil spirit was surrounded by the water and was compelled to remain in the cave of rocks for all time and his moanings are heard ever above the soft winds which at all times prevail over Ga-sa-qua-ji-mai-gog-sa-ga-ai-gan, now known as Leech Lake! This is how Leech Lake was formed. The Indian maiden escaped in a frail birch canoe that came floating from the shore one day. The land on which she climbed is pointed out as Bear Island.[2]

Earth scientists have a much less romantic legend of the origin of Leech Lake which tells about a series of glaciers that covered Minnesota - with strange names such as "Pliestocene" - and which were formed by heavy snows that melted only slightly in the summer months and therefore accumulated over the years until they were as much as one mile high! This legend then speaks of a changing, warming climate which melted the ice and snow and tells us that as the ice masses retreated they ground and gorged - boulder against boulder - forming hills and valleys, plains and lakes. When the last ice had melted away to a watery trickle, the area we now know as Leech Lake must have been quite un-beautiful - looking more like a moonscape. But then came vegetation and wildlife and the beauty which now inspires us.

The Ojibway named the lake, and "Leech" is a somewhat loose translation of their word for "blood sucker." The French called it Lac Sangsue and Jonathan Carver named it "White Deer" on his map - drawn in the 1760's.

We don't know how long the present shape and shoreline have been discernible but estimates run as high as 4000 years. The last dramatic change came with the construction of the dam at the northeast corner of the Lake in 1884, which raised the level seven feet. As a result, many of the original village sites now lie under water.

EARLY SETTLERS

Among the first inhabitants of the lake were probably the Laurel and the Blackduck peoples of the Woodland Culture. We think the Gros Ventre tribe was also here, and

[1] This was no idle boast. Only the bravest of the Ojibway drove the fearless Dakotas from their Leech Lake strongholds, and then dared to settle the area with their families during generations of counterattacks by the Sioux.

[2] Brochure, Walker Chamber of Commerce.

probably the Mandans. They were followed by the Dakotas in the 1600's and then the Ojibway.

Because of the nomadic nature of the early Indians, we can safely assume that many different tribes and family groups called Leech Lake "home" over a period of several thousands of years. They left behind only their dead and a few samples of their tools, weapons, and pottery. Just one example is a village site on Ricebed Point on the west side of Sucker Bay (now under water) which has revealed a culture which decorated the *inside* of its pottery - particularly the lips of the vessels - perhaps to bless the ingredients as they were poured from the pots over the design. When white men first came to this part of our country he found the Sioux in control of our entire woodlands region - with the exception of areas along the border. We really don't know exactly how long they had been here but it may have been for a hundred or more years. We believe the Sioux tribes moved into our state about 1000 A.D., but probably were not in control of Leech Lake until the 1600's.

As we have already read, the Ojibway were also on the move in the 17th century. They were being pushed west as a result of their losing confrontation with the allied tribes of the Iroquois Lodge. Although the Sioux and Algonquins were traditional enemies, the first contacts in the 1600's were quite peaceful; we have seen, in fact, how the Ojibway acted as middlemen between the French and the Dakotas in the fur trade business. But we also know that this relationship deteriorated in the 1700's and that all-out warfare was in full swing following the Sioux massacre of La Vérendrye's men on Lake of the Woods in 1736. Whole armies were still on the move in the Leech Lake area as late as 1768, and sizable bands of Dakotas continued to threaten the Leech Lake Ojibways almost up to the time of the Sioux uprising in southern Minnesota in 1862. Nor did the Treaty of Prairie du Chein in 1825 completely resolve the hostilities between the Ojibway and the Dakotas, although that was its intention.

But now let us look at the more specific and historic role Leech Lake played in this important era of Minnesota history.[1] At the time of the Lake of the Woods massacre, the Sioux had probably been on Leech Lake for about a hundred years. Giving it up - ever - was the farthest from their minds. We have no knowledge of exactly when or how the Dakotas gained control of this region; it is possible that it took quite some time and considerable bloodshed. No tribe would give it up without a fight. Not only was the lake strategically located, but it also had so much to offer as a sustainer of life. The lake itself had a generous population of fish. Early white explorers were particularly impressed with the size of the whitefish and compared them in quality to those in Lake Superior. They were also impressed with the muskellunge and described them as "three and four feet long." Rice beds were scattered around the lake, along the shores of the rivers which flow in and out of Leech, and also were in abundance on dozens of other lakes easily accessible by water. Its forests abounded with all manner of wildlife - firsthand sources of meat, hides, and furs. Berry patches were scattered throughout the pines and the maple hardwoods offered one of the best sources of sugar in the state. In the early years, Leech was reported to be host to a huge population of migratory waterfowl including ducks, geese, pelicans and swans. Goose Island and Pelican Island were so named because they were rookeries for these great birds. And all of the bounty forecast trouble. It is no wonder the Sioux would defend this land of

[1]It should be noted that much of the Minnesota Indian history of the 1700's and before is based on Ojibway tradition and is not historically documented. A great deal of the written account is the result of Warren's conversations with the old Chiefs, some of which (particularly dates) have been questioned. However, to the best of the author's knowledge, nothing quoted from Warren in this book has been proven untrue.

"milk and honey" until they had to move for the safety of their families; and no wonder it was coveted by the Ojibway.

Nevertheless, in three short years following the Lake of the Woods massacre, the Dakotas were dislodged from all of their northern Minnesota strongholds - including Leech Lake.

The first attacks on Leech were not by the Ojibway, but by their allies the Crees and Assiniboins from the north. Launching their attack from their Lake of the Woods and boundary water villages, they drove down on the Red Lakes, Winnibigoshish, Cass, and then Leech. The Ojibway seemed almost reluctant at first to join battle. Perhaps it was because their leadership still felt a loyalty to the French and their pursuit of peace among the tribes. However, when they had once committed themselves, it was with a vengeance - as we shall see when we tell our tales of Mille Lacs and other lakes. The Dakota villages at Sandy Lake also were to fall to the Ojibway - and this site was to become the new capital of the Ojibway Nation. Located on the watershed between Lake Superior and the Mississippi lake region at the end of the Savanna portage, it was the key to control of the entire area.

Thus, by 1739, the Dakotas had fled from their lake area strongholds and had moved their families to the prairies, and back into the southern part of the state - particularly along the Minnesota River. The once powerful Mille Lacs village of Kathio -what was left of it - was moved to the mouth of the Rum River. But the war was by no means over. It was really the beginning of a hundred year's war. No sooner would the Sioux be driven from an area than they would plan a counterattack. If the Ojibway or their allies moved out of an area, the Dakotas moved back in. Sometimes old village sites were even resettled by the original Sioux families. Although the Dakotas had been driven from their strongholds, they certainly had not given up; nor were the Ojibway and their allies strong enough to occupy and control the area. When villages were first established by the Ojibway and their allies, they were often wiped out - women, children and all. All of northern Minnesota soon became a virtual "no man's land" inhabited mostly by marauding war parties. The bands were not large - usually less than 100 braves in number. From 1739 to 1766, few tried to "live" in the area, and all who entered did so with intent to wage war. But when the ice went out of the lakes in the spring of 1766, the Ojibway organized an army of about 400 warriors from their villages along Lake Superior and throughout Wisconsin. When the war party left Fond du Lac it was said that a man standing on a high hill could not see the end or the beginning of the line formed by the Indians walking in single file - as was their custom.

By mid-May, the better-armed Ojibways had met and soundly defeated a much larger "army" of Dakotas, perhaps as many as 600 braves. The Dakotas at first fell back to Leech Lake and solidified their forces. Their first strategy was to occupy the islands of the lake. If they had been content to wait it out here until reinforcements arrived, they would have been relatively safe and could have held out for some time. However, over eager and over confident, the Dakotas made a grave error in strategy. They divided their forces and launched three simultaneous attacks on Pembina, Rainy Lake and Sandy Lake. They lost on all three fronts and the resultant disaster was the turning point of the war. The Sioux fell back to their villages west of the Mississippi and along the Minnesota River. The Dakota stronghold remained at the mouth of the Rum River.

The Ojibway were for the first time truly in control of the lake region and a serious effort was made to settle the area. Sandy Lake continued as the headquarters for their operations but villages soon appeared on the Red Lakes, Winnibigoshish, Cass Lake, Leech Lake, and Mille Lacs. Just as the islands of Leech Lake had been the last strongholds of the Dakotas they became the first homes of the Ojibway in the area. For even though the Ojibway had effectively defeated the Dakotas, Sioux war parties would return again and again for many years to view their old village sites, visit the burial places of their ancestors, and administer vengeance to the Ojibways. In fact, if the Ojibway villages had not been replenished continuously with settlers from the east, they surely would have been annihilated.

One such raid by several hundred Dakota warriors occurred in 1768 and originated at the Sioux village at the mouth of the Rum River. The small army traveled north up the Mississippi, then took the Crow Wing cut-off up Gull River, through Gull and Whitefish, up Pine River, then through a series of portages to Leech Lake. Their target was Sandy Lake, but it is likely that many of the newly arrived Ojibway settlers fell victim along the way including those on Leech Lake. When they arrived at Sandy Lake they found only women, children, and old men. By a tragic coincidence, the Ojibway warriors were away on a raid of their own - at the mouth of the Rum River - the home of the Dakota invaders! The two war parties had missed each other because the Ojibway had traveled down the Mississippi all the way while the Sioux took the Crow Wing cut-off. The Dakotas devasted the Ojibway village - taking 30 young women as slaves plus one older woman to care for them and killing everyone else. As the Dakota party started south the Ojibway party moved north. They were destined to meet in an historic battle - but that is another story more appropriately saved for our tales of the Crow Wing River.

A NEW ENEMY

During the time of the American Revolution, the raids and counter raids continued. But in 1782 - one year after victory came for the colonies - the native people met a new enemy - more sinister and devastating than any war party. This new foe was destined to kill a far greater total number than any of the Sioux-Algonquin wars. It was an enemy with which the Indian could not cope. It was the unseen germ that caused a disease called "smallpox."

According to one legend,[1] the new Ojibway villages at Leech Lake played a significant role in bringing the disease to the Minnesota lake region. Because of the inter-tribal wars, no trader had ventured into the area for many years (perhaps more than forty). In the spring of 1781, a trader, accompanied by a handful of voyageurs, traveled up the Mississippi. He chose the Crow Wing cut-off and camped at the mouth of Pillager Creek.[2] Here he took ill (not smallpox) and was forced to rest. A band of Leech Lake Ojibway - perhaps out to make sure there were no Sioux war parties in the area, came across the sick trader and his men. Upon seeing his goods they were most anxious to do business; after all, for more than a generation they had been forced to travel to La Pointe, Grand Portage, Ontario, or Mackinac to do their trading. The trader, however, was too ill to do business. But the Indians were not to be denied. As the story goes, they at first intended to leave items of equal value to those taken, but

[1] Warren, William, History of the Ojibways.

[2] According to one legend, the Leech Lake band of Ojibway Indians received the name "Pillagers" because of the "pillaging" which took place here. Other legends say "Pillager" is a translation of the name other Indians gave them because of their aggressiveness: "Muk-im-dua-win-in-e-wing," meaning "men who take by force."

when a cask of "firewater" was discovered and consumed, their judgement was clouded. As matters grew worse, the voyageurs placed the trader in his canoe and headed back down river. The next day, near the present site of Sauk Rapids, the trader died.

When the news reached the Ojibway leadership on Leech Lake, there was much consternation. Now, they feared, it would be many more years before a trader would again venture into their area. Thus it was, that the next year, 1782, a delegation was sent from Leech Lake to Mackinac - then a British fort - to make amends. Their peace offering of furs was well received and the English gave them in return a bale of goods, a British flag (assuming correctly, that the Indians had not yet learned the colonies had won the war), and a coat and medal for their chief. On their return trip, the happy Leech Lake delegation stopped at Fond du Lac and proudly displayed their goods. They may have been contaminated with smallpox germs. In a matter of days the village was all but wiped out by the dread disease - including the leader of the Leech Lake group. Survivors fled, carrying the disease with them to all parts of the lake region. According to the legend, the British had instructed the Indians not to open their goods until they had returned to their village. Some hold this as evidence that the English had planted contaminated goods; others say the instructions were given because the English had lost the war and by displaying the flag someone might inform the Indians of the outcome, thus making them less inclined to cooperate with the English. At any rate, the plague was spread by this incident. However, by the time the Leech Lake Indians had returned to their villages, the disease had apparently run its course and the Leech area itself was not as severely affected as other villages.

It is also believed that smallpox entered Minnesota from the west.[1] The carriers in this case were a party of Assiniboins, Cree, and Ojibway who had come upon a village in North Dakota[2] - either Mandans or Gros Ventres - which was experiencing a smallpox devastation. There was little resistance, and the war party took many scalps. When they returned to the boundary waters with their infected trophies they spread the disease across what is now northern Minnesota and into Ontario. Some historians believe this may have been the source of infection in Fond du Lac and that it arrived simultaneously with the Leech Lake Indians returning from Mackinac.

Whatever the source, the devastation was beyond present-day comprehension. The huge village at Sandy Lake was reduced to seven wigwams. Other villages were even less fortunate; sometimes there were no survivors. Jean Baptiste Cadotte, the French trader, sent this only slightly exaggerated message to Mackinac: "All the Indians from Fond du Lac, Rainy Lake, Sandy Lake, and surrounding places are dead from smallpox."

But all did not die, and the villages were eventually repopulated.

TRAINING GROUND FOR LEADERSHIP

The Leech Lake area produced a remarkable number of outstanding Ojibway leaders (and probably Sioux before them).

Why?

It may have been because the tribes fought so hard to possess the lake and then to hang on to it. Perhaps it was that for nearly a century only the bravest tried to "settle" this "no man's land." It may have been because of the concern and heartache the

[1]Zapffe, Carl A., "The Man Who Lived in Three Centuries."
[2]See page 17.

Ojibway experienced as white settlers, loggers and Indian agents moved in. Whatever the reason, there was a disproportionate measure of leadership to the population of the area - even though Leech eventually boasted one of the largest settlements of Ojibway people.

The Indian population on Leech Lake prior to the epidemic was reported as about "100 warriors." In 1832, Henry Schoolcraft estimated a total population of 800; four years later, Nicollet reported 1000 inhabitants on the lake; and in 1851 the payment census list included one thousand two hundred fifty names.

Most Leech Lake Pillagers were of the Bear and Catfish totems.

CHIEFS OF THE 1700's

Among the chiefs who had prominent roles in driving the Dakotas from the lake region of Minnesota were:

Bi-aus-wa, generally accepted as the leader of the first successful attacks on Sandy Lake. He was the principal chief of the Sandy Lake village during its first years as capital of the Ojibway Nation. Bi-aus-wa was even better known, however, for his civil leadership than as a war chief.

Noka, a war chief who fought under Bi-aus-wa's leadership and for whom the Nokasippi was named. He was grandfather of the Waub-o-jeeg of the 19th century. Noka was a leader of the Ojibway war party of 200 braves which wiped out a Sioux village near the mouth of the Minnesota River in retaliation for the destruction of the Sandy Lake village. When the Ojibway left the north country the ice was just out and there were no leaves on the trees. They were surprised to find the trees in full leaf farther south and for that reason gave the name "Osh-ke-bug-e-sebe" or "New Leaf River" to the stream we now call the Minnesota River.

Waus-e-ko-gubigs, or "Bright Forehead," grandfather of Flat Mouth, who was destined to become Leech Lake's most distinguished chieftain.

Wa-son-aun-e-qua, or "Yellow Hair," father of Flat Mouth. According to his illustrious son, Yellow Hair achieved his power through his knowledge of medicines and poisons. He hunted the area around Long Prairie, where he lost three children in an attack by the Sioux. He gained revenge by killing and wounding several Dakotas and scalping alive a girl offered to him as a replacement for his own lost children.

Kechi-wa-bi-she-shi, or "Great Marten," who when killed near Elk River was said to have fought in nearly 100 battles and been wounded in many of them. He was Bi-aus-wah's most important war chief and lead every major campaign against the Sioux after the Ojibway and settled in the northern lake region of Minnesota.

Waub-o-jeeg I, or "White Fisher," the Ojibway leader who not only drove the Sioux from the Wisconsin lake region (Battle of St. Croix Falls) but also the Sauk and the Fox - both Algonquin tribes which had allied themselves with the Dakotas. He not only earned a reputation in Minnesota but also made the Minnesota invasion possible by securing northern Wisconsin for the Ojibways.

Uk-ke-waus, who was not really a chief but who led a reluctant band of forty-five Leech Lake warriors on a raid of Sioux villages in the Leaf Lakes and Battle Lake area. At the outset, the majority of Leech Lake Indians were anxious to organize a war party against the Sioux. Jean Baptiste Cadotte (son of the Cadotte who was one of the first men to have contact with the Ojibways) had established a trading post at Cass Lake. When the Pillagers came to him for powder and shot, he pursuaded them not to go on the warpath. However, when they returned to Leech Lake with some firewater, a wild celebration was held. The next morning, Uk-ke-waus dared the braves to follow him on a mission of revenge against the Sioux. Of the forty-five who answered his call, less than one-third returned. In a violent battle at Battle Lake (from which the lake received its name), Uk-ke-waus and all four of his sons were killed. He and his three oldest sons had fought to their death in a delaying action against a large number of Dakotas so that the handful of remaining Ojibways might escape.[1]

Flat Mouth, who was a young man at the time, joined a group of Uk-ke-waus' Red Lake relatives in a raid west to the prairies. Flat Mouth recalled in his later years that they had a measure of revenge and told how they set out on showshoes from Red Lake but were able to travel on bare ground once they reached the prairies. He also told of encountering enormous herds of buffalo.[1]

TWO EXAMPLES OF 18TH CENTURY BATTLES BETWEEN THE OJIBWAY AND THE DAKOTAS.[1]

Great Marten (Keche-wa-bi-she-shi), whom we have described as Bi-aus-wa's great war chief who lead every major raid from the Sandy Lake-Leech Lake area against the Sioux, perhaps deserves more credit than any other man for maintaining Ojibway control of the Minnesota lake region. It is appropriate, therefore, that we have chosen his two last campaigns as examples of Indian warfare during the late 1700's and early 1800's as the Dakotas and Ojibway contested for control of our state.

The first campaign - under Great Marten's leadership - originated at Sandy Lake and included about 120 braves. It would be fair to speculate that some of the warriors might have come from the Leech-Cass Lake area, inasmuch as it was customary to invite participation from neighboring villages when large parties were organized. A runner was sometimes sent from village to village bearing something symbolic belonging to the leader, such as a pipe or tomahawk - along with an invitation to join the campaign.

By the time of this first incursion, the Mississippi had become the favorite warpath of the Ojibway in their attempts to expand their frontiers to the south and make their lake region villages more safe from Sioux attack. As the war party proceeded down the river, Great Marten sent a canoe of scouts ahead and runners along each bank to make certain there would be no ambush. A short distance above the mouth of the Elk River, the scouts heard voices of the Dakotas dialect. Quickly and silently they turned their canoe, moved in tight to the shoreline, and worked their way back upstream without detection. When they came in sight of their main party they threw water up in the air with their paddles to signify danger and that the war party should turn in to the eastern bank. After quickly applying war paint and adorning their hair with eagle feathers,[2] they ran in disorder through the wooded river bottoms until they came to the open prairie. Before them was a line of Dakota warriors in battle dress, apparently starting on the warpath against some northern Ojibway destination. Great Marten's men, all "psyched-up" for battle, charged out onto the prairie. When the parties were

[1]Warren, William, "History of the Ojibway," Vol. 5, Minnesota Historical Collection.
[2]Each Eagle plume represented a slain enemy or a scalp taken in battle.

in gun range of each other they opened fire. Because there was no cover, the only defense was to keep in motion. It must have been a spectacular sight - the painted and plumed bodies leaping continually from side to side - accented by war whoops and gun fire. Although the two bands were about equal in size, the late arriving Ojibways kept pouring from the woods and the Dakotas, assuming they would soon be badly outnumbered, turned and fled, leaving behind their blankets and other paraphernalia they were carrying for their raid in the north. A running flight continued for about three miles, when the Dakotas met a large party from another Dakota village, apparently on their way to join them in their campaign against the Ojibway. Now the tide turned and Great Marten's braves took flight. Upon reaching a grove of oak trees they made a stand. The Sioux were without cover and dug holes in the ground (fox holes are not an innovation of our times) and so the battle continued. As the Sioux tried to dig in closer they suffered numerous casualties. Then, noting a stiff south wind and the dry prairie grass killed during the recent winter, the Dakotas set a fire. The Ojibway were soon routed from the oak grove and lost three of their number to the encircling flames. The prairie fire did, however, give them time to flee to the river and take refuge on an island. Although the battle continued for some time, an impasse was reached and the war-weary Indians finally returned to their respective villages. The Ojibways claimed the Dakotas had suffered severe losses but admitted to losing eight warriors in addition to the three lost in the fire. Since the Ojibway were recognized as superior marksmen (they may have been using guns for more years than the Sioux) it is entirely possible that the report is fairly accurate.

The following year, Great Marten lead a second campaign down the Mississippi. This time the war party was smaller in number - about sixty braves. At exactly the same spot where the Ojibway had fought the Dakotas the previous year, they again encountered a war party. But this time the invaders were seriously outnumbered - estimates ran as high as 400 Dakotas. Overnight, Great Marten's warriors dug in, taking time to dig fox holes up to three feet deep which would hold one or two men. The Dakotas, meanwhile, had taken possession of a wooded area in range of the Ojibway. Even though the Sioux completely outnumbered the Ojibway, they were in no hurry to sacrifice their men with an open charge. Occasionally, a more daring brave would make a move and pay for it with his life. Then an equally brave (or foolish) enemy would dash out from cover to secure the scalp. Others would try to retrieve the body to prevent mutilation (which many believed could adversely effect the fallen brave's after-life). Hand to hand skirmishes resulted. On one such foray Great Marten - who had tempted death on scores of occasions over the years - lost his life. The Sioux had also suffered losses and that night retreated some distance. The Ojibway, discouraged and saddened by the loss of their leader, returned to their canoes under the shelter of darkness and headed for the north country.

The point of land between the Elk and Mississippi Rivers - where both battles were fought - was thereafter called "Me-gaud-e-win-ing" or "Battle Ground."

It is difficult to comprehend the dangers and uncertainties of living in Minnesota during this hundred year period. Not only was there open warfare with muskets - not just bows and arrows - but no village, no hunter, not even the women and children gathering wild rice or maple sap were safe from the marauding bands of Ojibway and Dakota warriors.

AMONG THE PILLAGER CHIEFS WHO HEADQUARTERED AT LEECH LAKE DURING THE 1800's WERE:

Eshke-bog-e-coshe, called "Gueule Platte" by the French traders and "Flat Mouth"[1] by the English and Americans. Literally, the French words are translated: platte - meaning flat, and gueule - meaning the mouth of an animal. So the expression was hardly intended to be complimentary.

Born in the early 1770's, after the Sioux had been routed from their lake region strongholds, Flat Mouth's leadership came during a time when the major concern was holding Leech Lake against Dakota attacks. White explorers and traders quickly recognized him as the most influential chief on the lake.

Flat Mouth saw, and was a part of, the years of historic development of our state. When the Pike Expedition reached Leech Lake in 1805, he was already a powerful chief. In 1812, when the British tried to persuade the Ojibway to join them in their war against the United States, it was Flat Mouth who said "no" and whose leadership was a factor in keeping 99 percent of the Minnesota Ojibway loyal to the American "Long Knives." In 1832, when Henry Schoolcraft visited Leech, he was older but no less powerful. When the time came for negotiations and treaties with the United States Government, it was Flat Mouth who represented the Leech Lake area Pillagers. Several times he was brought to Washington D.C., and on one occasion posed for the magnificant piece of sculpture still on display in the United States Capitol (one of only three Indians so honored). His life spanned our nation's formative years between the Revolution and the Civil War. Flat Mouth's village was located on Otter Tail Point by the north narrows. This was almost as easily defended as one of the islands.

When necessary, Flat Mouth was a man of war. He not only defended his home base, but he participated in a number of raids against the Sioux. He joined with "Curly Head," the first great Ojibway Chieftain at Gull Lake, in a raid on a Sioux Village near Long Prairie to avenge the death of his nephew and also of two popular Ojibway leaders and warriors - Waub-o-jeeg II (namesake of the famous Wisconsin Chief of the previous century) and She-shebe (hero of the Cross Lake massacre). After nearly wiping out the entire village, a handful of brave Sioux kept them from taking scalps. But the Dakotas moved out following this defeat and never again attempted to establish a permanent village in the Long Prairie area. But mostly, Flat Mouth was a man of peace. Although loyal to the United States he grew uneasy and unhappy with white intrusions, yet, his contributions were many in the peaceful and orderly early development of the lake region of Minnesota.

Kechi Osaye, or "Elder Brother," was a contemporary of Flat Mouth and considered an ally. Although he held the rank of chief and ruled over his own village, he was not as powerful as Flat Mouth and held a secondary position in the heirarchy. W.T. Boutwell, a Presbyterian missionary who accompanied Henry Schoolcraft to Leech Lake in 1832 and who returned the next year to establish a mission school on the shores of Trader Bay, described Elder Brother as "An Indian among a thousand for his sincerity, integrity, and inflexible love of truth and equity. He is the most worthy Indian I have ever met . . ."

Maji-gabo, who as described by Henry Schoolcraft when he met him at Leech Lake in 1832, as "tall, gaunt and savage looking." The description fits his reputation well. In

[1]There were several chiefs by this name; this Chief is known to historians as Flatmouth I or Flatmouth the elder.

AYSH-KE-BAH-KE-KO-ZHAY.
(FLAT-MOUTH.)
A CHIPPEWA CHIEF.

Eshke-bog-e-coshe (Flat-Mouth) of Leech Lake. Bust by Francis Vincenti. Location: Senate wing, third floor, east. (One of only three Indian statues in the U.S. Capitol).

Pe-zhe-Ke or "Buffalo." His wisdom saved many white lives.

division was serious; the Dakotas were too great a common enemy.

   Pe-zhe-ke, or Buffalo, who was among those Leech Lake chieftains who inherited some of the prestige and power of Flat Mouth following his death. In 1862, the year of the great Sioux uprisings and massacres in southern Minnesota, the Ojibway were planning an uprising of their own in northern Minnesota. Many believe there was an alliance between Little Crow - the legendary Dakota Chief - and Hole-in-the-Day of the Ojibways. The Leech Lake Pillagers were anxious to join in the Ojibway uprising and there is every reason to believe that if the younger braves had prevailed there would have been a great loss of life among the scattered white settlers of the lake region. The Leech Indians were expected to join Hole-in-the-Day at the isthmus of land between Round and Gull Lakes (along with war parties from all over the lake area.) Before leaving for the appointed rendezvous, zealous Leech Lake braves captured the handful of Whites in the area and prepared to put them to death. Chief Buffalo and Chief Big Dog (who had also inherited some of Flat Mouth's influence) argued that it would be better to take them along alive to Gull Lake just in case something had gone wrong with Hole-in-the-Day's plans and then they would be left "holding the bag" as murderers of white men. Fortunately, their logic prevailed, because, as we shall learn from our tales of Gull Lake, the uprising was aborted.

Kechi-Ani-mos, or "Big Dog," as we have already indicated, was contemporary with Chief Buffalo and helped stop short a move to massacre the Whites in the area and then join with Chief Hole-in-the-Day in a general uprising which was to have originated at Gull Lake.

Negona-pin-ay-se, which means "Leading Bird," but who assumed the name of his deceased father and became Flat Mouth II. Although he inherited his father's mantle he earned the respect of his people in his own right and was of considerable influence among the Leech Lake Pillagers for the rest of the century.

Kay-gway-jaway-benung, or Maji-gabo II, or "Red Blanket," who was the son of the original Maji-gabo, the renowned war chief of Flat Mouth's day. He was the Chief of the Bear Island Pillagers at the time of the historic 1898 Leech Lake uprising.

Pugona-geshig,[1] or "Hole-in-the-Day of Leech Lake," who was "affectionately" named "Old Bug" by the whites. It was his refusal to submit to a subpoena that lead to the last Indian war in the United States, in 1898. We shall hear more of his story later. He was a brother of Red Blanket.

Kechi-Way-mitig-ozbe, or "Great Frenchman." He was a half-brother to Chief Wa-bo-se and to Chief Mitig-gwah-kik-ens (Drum Beater) of Lake Pokegama. Great Frenchman was granted the title of "chief" by Flat Mouth I because of the death of one of his sons at the hands of one of Flat Mouth's sons. He is best remembered as the father of John Smith, "the man who lived in three centuries"[2] - perhaps the oldest person to have ever lived in our state.

HISTORIC VISITS TO LEECH LAKE IN THE 1800's

Lieutenant Zebulon Pike

In 1805, Pike journeyed up the Mississippi in search of the source of the river. He was formally commissioned by General James Wilkinson (sometimes suspected of treasonous intent because of his friendship with Aaron Burr) to explore and take possession of the country and to gain permission from the Indians to construct a military fort and trading houses at strategic locations. Pike's subsequent negotiations with the Sioux were particularly significant in Minnesota history because Fort Snelling was later constructed on property secured as a result of the agreement reached with the Sioux.

The United States Government was aware of the fact that the British operated Northwest Company was still trading in the area. One of Pike's assignments was to advise the chief traders of these posts that duty must be paid on goods brought into our country (at Mackinac) and that they could no longer fly the British flag. In early winter Pike proceeded up the river but was forced to call a halt because of icing conditions on the Mississippi - about thirty miles south of its confluence with the Crow

---

[1]Some consider the Pioute rebellion of the 1920's and the recent Wounded Knee conflicts as later Indian Wars.
[2]Zapffe, Carl A., "The Man Who Lived in Three Centuries," Historic Heartland Association, P.O. Box 1, Brainerd, Minnesota. The author traces much of the early history of our state through the long life of John Smith of Cass Lake, Minnesota.

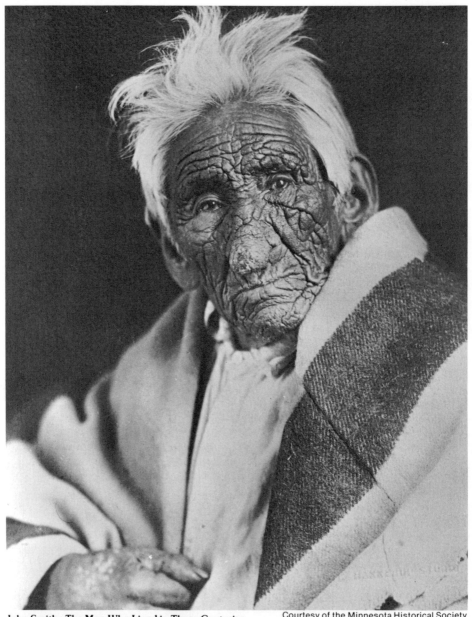

John Smith - The Man Who Lived in Three Centuries.   Courtesy of the Minnesota Historical Society

Wing (Pike Rapids).[1] Later that winter he proceeded, with his company of soldiers, to Leech Lake. The winter was apparently at first quite mild because the river ice proved unsafe. Much of the journey had to be over-land; even so, sleds broke through ice on more than one occasion. Powder that was not stored in water-proof kegs had to be dried. The men barely escaped serious injury or death when the powder, being dried in iron kettles near a fire, blew up! At one point Pike's tent caught on fire and the powder stored there had to be hastily removed. Extreme cold set in, followed by nearly three feet of snow, and the troops were forced to stop about every three miles to build fires. In spite of all the hardships, the Northwest post at Sandy Lake was finally reached; after a rest, they continued on to Leech Lake. At Leech he found a Northwest Company trading post, surrounded by a stockade, and located on Ottertail Point, two miles from Flatmouth's village and across from Goose Island. This post was also under English control and the chiefs of the area were proud possessors of British flags and medals. Although cordially received and feasted with baked beaver and boiled moose head, Lt. Pike ordered the British flag shot down and replaced it with the stars and stripes. In a ceremony on February 16, 1806, he claimed the area in the name of the United States government. The Indians placed great significance on the occasion and exchanged their medals and flags for those of our country. Flat Mouth, who was present at the ceremony, observed that on that day he "ceased to be an Englishman and became a Long Knife" (as the Indians referred to the Americans). "Trader Anderson" was also on the lake in 1805. He is thought to have been working under the British agent and independent Trader, Col. Robert Dickson, and to have been located on Squaw Point. Anderson actually spent many years trapping and trading in the Minnesota-Wisconsin area.

Pike was fully aware of the Ojibway-Sioux hostilities and did his best to establish peace in the region. In his opening speech at Leech Lake he said, "I was chosen to ascend the Mississippi to bear to his red children the words of their father, and the Great Spirit has opened the eyes and ears of all the nations to listen to my words. The Sauks and Reynards are planting corn and raising cattle. The Winnebagos continue peaceable as usual, and even the Sioux have laid by the hatchet at my request. Yes, my brothers, the Sioux who have so long and obstinately warred against the Chippeways, have agreed to lay by the hatchet, smoke the calumet, and again become your brothers. Brothers! You behold the pipe of Wabasha as a proof of what I say. The Little Corbeau, Fils de Pinchon, and L'Aile Roughe, had marched two hundred and fifty warriors to revenge the blood of their women and children, slain last year at the St. Peters.[2] I sent a runner after them, stopped their march, and met them in council at the mouth of the St. Peters, where they promised to remain peaceable until my return; and if the Ouchipawah chiefs accompanied me, to receive them as brothers, and accompany us to St. Louis, there to bury the hatchet, and smoke the pipe in the presence of our great war-chief; and to request him to punish those who first broke the peace . . . Brothers! I understand that one of your young men killed an American at Red Lake last year, but that the murderer is far off; let him keep so; send him where we may never hear of him more, for were he here I would be obliged to demand him of you, and make my young men shoot him."

A Red Lake Indian Chief "Old Sweet" was present, and responded thus, "My father! I have heard and understood the words of our great father. It overjoys me to

[1]During recent low water, traces may be seen from the air of what might have been the perimeters of Pike's camp.
[2]The Minnesota River.

see you make peace among us. I should have accompanied you had my family been present, and would have gone to see their father, the great war-chief.

"The medal I hold in my hand I received from the English chiefs. I willingly deliver it up to you. Wabasha's calumet with which I am presented, I receive with all my heart. Be assured that I will use my best endeavors to keep my young men quiet. There is my calumet, I send it to my father the great war-chief. What does it signify that I should go to see him?

"My father! you will meet the Sioux on your return. You may make them smoke in my pipe, and tell them that I have let fall my hatchet.

"My father! tell the Sioux on the upper part of the St. Peters River, that they mark trees with the figure of a calumet, that we of Red Lake who go that way, should we see them, may make peace with them, being assured of their pacific disposition, when we shall see the calumet marked on the trees."

Flat Mouth gave similar assurances and designated his brother, Beau, and another chief called "The Buck" as personal emissaries to travel with Pike to visit the Sioux and then go on to St. Louis.

Pike was eventually promoted to brigadier general and died a hero's death in the war of 1812. Pike's peak in Colorado and Pike's Bay of Cass Lake honor his name.

BRITISH AGENTS INVITE THE PILLAGERS TO JOIN THEM IN THE WAR OF 1812

Although several Canadian Ojibway tribes aligned themselves with the British in the War of 1812, virtually none of the Minnesota Ojibway joined the English. However, every effort was made by the British to recruit the Minnesota Indians. Col. Robert Dickson,[1] who had made a career of trading with the Dakotas and the northern Ojibway, was perhaps the best known of the British agents who tried to persuade the Indians to fight against the Americans. He sent an interpreter by the name of St. Germain to Leech Lake to deliver presents and waumpum belts to Flat Mouth as the most influential chief. A public meeting was held and Flat Mouth said (in later years to William Warren) that he had responded thus, "When I go to war against my enemies, I do not call on the Whites to join my warriors. The white people have quarrelled among themselves, and I do not wish to meddle in their quarrels, nor do I intend ever, even to be guilty of breaking the windowglass of a white man's dwelling."

Wabasha, a hereditary Sioux Chief joined forces with Dickson; so did Joseph Renville - a Sioux half-breed and noted guide and interpreter who had served with Pike. Dickson and his Indian allies captured Mackinac without a shot, also Fort Shelby at Prairie du Chien.

Henry Schoolcraft - 1820 and 1832

Schoolcraft had been chosen by Governor Lewis Cass (of the Michigan Territory) as a member of his 1820 expedition up the Mississippi for the following purposes as he had set them forth in a letter to Secretary of War Calhoun; "with a view to examine the production of its animal, vegetable, and mineral kingdoms, to explore its facilities for water communication, to delineate its natural objects, and to ascertain its present and future probable value . . ." At that time, Schoolcraft was known as an author and

[1]Dickson operated independently of the Hudson's Bay and Northwest Co. He and his partners operated posts at the mouth of the Rum River, Sauk Rapids, and the mouth of the Minnesota, as well as on Leech Lake.

mineralogist. The 1820's Expedition apparently terminated at a lake Pike had called "Upper Red Cedar;" Schoolcraft renamed it "Cassina," in honor of the Governor. Today we call it "Cass Lake," and the lower lake we have named "Pike Bay."

In 1832, Schoolcraft was an Indian Agent, and he organized his own expedition. As we know, he successfully identified Lake Itasca as the true source of the Mississippi River. Late on July 16th, accompanied by an escort of soldiers (under the command of Lt. James Allen) and Rev. William T. Boutwell (a Presbyterian missionary who was then stationed at Mackinac) Schoolcraft arrived at Leech Lake. Rev. Boutwell gives us a remarkable picture of an aging Flat Mouth in his report of the event in the Boston "Missionary Herald" in 1834: "the principal chief (Flat Mouth) sent his "Mishinne," waiting-man, requesting Mr. Schoolcraft to come and breakfast with him.

"Decorum required him to comply with the request, though he was at liberty to furnish the table mostly himself. A mat spread in the middle of the floor served as a table, upon which the dishes were placed. Around this were spread others upon which the guests sat while the wife of the chief waited upon the table, and poured the tea. She afterward took breakfast by herself." After breakfast they proceeded to the Chief's headquarters which was thus described: "It is a building perhaps twenty feet by twenty-five, made of logs, which I am informed was presented to him by one of the traders. As we entered, the old chief, bare-legged and bare-foot, sat with much dignity upon a cassette. A blanket, and cloth about the loins, covered his otherwise naked body, which was painted black. His chief men occupied a bench by his side, while forty or more of his warriors sat on the floor around the walls of his room smoking. The old man arose and gave us his hand as we were introduced, bidding us to take a seat at his right, on his bed. As I cast my eye around upon his savage group, for once, I wished I possessed the painter's skill. The old chief had again returned to his seat upon the large wooden trunk, and as if to sit a little more like a white man than an Indian, had thrown one leg across the other knee. His warriors were all feathered, painted, and equipped for service. Many of them wore the insignia of courage, a strip of polecat skin around the head or heels, the bushy tail of the latter so attached as to drag on the ground; the crown of the head was ornamented with feathers, indicating the number of enemies the individual had killed, on one of which I counted no less than twelve.

"One side of his room was hung with an English and American flag, medals, war-clubs, lances, tomahawks, arrows, and other implements of death. The subject of vaccination was now presented to the chief, with which he was pleased, and ordered his people to assemble for that purpose. I stood by the doctor, and kept the minutes while he performed the business.

"Preparations were now made for taking our leave when the chief arose, and giving his hand to each, spoke as follows, in reply to Mr. Schoolcraft, who had addressed them as 'My children.' 'You call us children. We are not children, but men. When I think of the condition of my people I can hardly refrain from tears. It is so melancholy that even the trees weep over it. When I heard that you were coming to visit us, I felt inclined to go and meet you. I hoped that you would bring us relief. But if you did not furnish some relief, I thought I should go farther, to the people who wear big hats, in hopes of obtaining that relief from them, which the Long Knives (Americans) have so often promised.

Our great Father promised us, when we smoked the pipe with the Sioux at Prairie du Shien in 1825, and at Fond du Lac in 1826, that the first party who crossed the line, and broke the treaty, should be punished. This promise has not been fulfilled. Not a year has passed but some of our young men, our wives, and our children have fallen, and the blood that has begun to flow will not soon stop. I do not expect this year will close before more of my young men will fall. When my son was killed, about a year since, I determined not to lay down any arms as long as I can see the light of the sun. I do not think the Great Spirit ever made us to sit still and see our young men, our wives, and our children murdered.

'Since we have listened to the Long Knives, we have not prospered. They are not willing we should go ourselves, and flog our enemies, nor do they fulfill their promise and do it for us.'

"The medals of each chief and a string of wampum were now brought forth stained with vermilion.

"See our medals," and holding them up by the strings, he continued: "These and all your letters are stained with blood. I return them all to you to make them bright. None of us wish to receive them back," laying them at Mr. Schoolcraft's feet, "until you have wiped off the blood."

"Here a shout of approbation was raised by all his warriors present, and the old man, growing more eloquent, forgot that he was holding his blanket around his naked body with one hand, and it dropped from about him, and he proceeded: "The words of the Long Knives have passed through our forests as a rushing wind, but they have been words merely. They have only shaken the trees, but have not stopped to break them down, nor even to make the rough places smooth."

"It is not that we wish to be at war with the Sioux, but when they enter our country and kill our people, we are obliged to revenge their death. Nor will I conceal from you the fact that I have already sent tobacco and pipestems to different bands to invite them to come to our relief. We have been successful in the late war, but we do not feel that we have taken sufficient revenge.'

"Here a bundle of sticks two inches long was presented, indicating the number of Ojibways killed by the Sioux since the treaty of 1825, amounting to forty-three. Just as we were ready to embark, the old man came out in his regimentals, a military coat faced with red, ruffled shirt, hat, pantaloons, gloves, and shoes. So entirely changed was his appearance that I did not recognize him until he spoke."

When Schoolcraft arrived at Leech, he found an American Fur Company trading post located just east of Flat Mouth's village on Otter Tail Point. Some of the original Canadian traders were still on the lake (among them Rosseau) but operating under a license issued to John Fairbanks by the American Company. Aliens were not eligible for a license.

As we have already indicated, Boutwell returned to Leech Lake in 1833 and organized a Presbyterian mission school on Trader Bay. His diary tells of living in a wigwam and of great physical hardship.

Nicollet - 1836

Joseph Nicollet stopped at Leech Lake for one week in August on his way north to explore the upper Mississippi area, and again for a week on his way back in September. He spent considerable time with Missionary Boutwell and held extensive interviews with Chief Flat Mouth. Nicollet constructed a map of the lake and named "Pickering Bay" after John Pickering of Massachusetts in appreciation for his work with Indian languages.

At first the Indians threatened to deprive the small expedition of all its goods and perhaps would have, if Boutwell had not intervened.

The Indian Agency

In 1866 a sub-agency was established at Leech Lake and headquartered at Onigum. The following year what may have been the first boarding school for Indians in Minnesota was established here with a capacity for fifty scholars. In 1879 the Leech Lake, Red Lakes, and White Earth Reservations were combined with the principal headquarters at White Earth. The agent characterized the three bands in his annual report as "among the most self-supporting" in Minnesota. In 1899 the Red Lake and Leech agencies were again separated from White Earth; the headquarters was established at Leech Lake with Red Lake as a sub-agency. John Sutherland was the agent in charge. He was followed by Gustave Kulander, a great-great uncle of the author.

The author's mother spent several summers with her uncle at Onigum. In later years she told many stories indicating her displeasure with the paternalistic treatment and generally demeaning attitude towards the Indians served by the agency.

THE LAST OF THE INDIAN WARS[1]

If we were to ask someone from one of the eastern seaboard states where the last Indian uprising took place in our country - few would guess "Minnesota." But it is really not so surprising when we realize that northern Minnesota was about as underdeveloped in 1898 as any of the states of the West or Southwest.

The incident which brought troops to Leech Lake was in itself quite insignificant, and if a rifle had not fallen from its stacked position and accidentally discharged, there may have been no battle at all. However, the general discontent and restlessness of the Indians at that time made the incident possible. One might also speculate that the danger of a general Indian uprising across the lake region would have been much more likely except for the knowledge all Ojibways had of how the Sioux had been literally driven out of southern Minnesota fifteen years earlier following the massacres which had taken place in the New Ulm-Mankato area.

The center of the controversy was old Chief Pugona-geshig, called "Old Bug" by the whites. At the root of the problem was the illegal sale of liquor to the Indians. Government agents were seeking witnesses to convict "bootleggers" and "Old Bug" was being sought as such a witness for a trial which was to be held in Duluth. In his younger days, "Old Bug" had been taken to this same city for a similar purpose and was allegedly left to find his own way back to Leech Lake. As the story goes, he was twice thrown off trains. It was winter, and he endured many hardships, including freezing, before returning to his home on Leech. He vowed never again to be subjected to such treatment and this time he hid in the forest. Eventually he was forced to come out of hiding to report at the old agency in Trader Bay in order to collect his regular census payment. He simply could not forego what he thought was rightfully his. U.S. Marshals promptly arrested him; when he resisted, he was handcuffed. At first, other Indians were hesitant to interfere, but his cries for help and taunting words finally shamed some of the younger braves into attacking the marshals and roughing

[1]Recent action at Wounded Knee, South Dakota, and the Pioute uprisings in the 1920's could be considered as serious as the Leech Lake affair.

them up. "Old Bug" made for the woods but handicapped by his age and the shackels, he was caught again. This time a group of Indian women got into the act and "Old Bug" made good his escape. In the days that followed, a large number of Indians rallied to his support and the marshals, recognizing their own limitations and the gravity of the situation, requested military support.

Old Chief Pugona-geshig (on the left), nicknamed "Old Bug" (the Ojibway "P" is pronounced "B"). He was the focal point of the last white-Indian war in our country.

Courtesy of the Minnesota Historical Society

Law and order had to be maintained and a contingent of soldiers was sent north under the leadership of General John Bacon and Major Melville C. Wilkinson. The author's father, Richard Lund, was living in Brainerd at the time; although only eight years old, he had vivid recollections of the troop trains as they pulled into that city on their way to Walker. Even though local citizens were apprehensive, they generally made light of the situation and cheered the soldiers on their way. He also recalled the somewhat relieved but very sober crowd that greeted a returning train with its dead and wounded.

The first troop train arrived in September, the second just after the first of October, and a third came later. On the morning of October 5, 1898, General Bacon, Major Wilkinson, and about two hundred soldiers set out from Walker on barges, headed for Sugar Point (now also called Battle Point) where the fugitive had his cabin home and a garden. The soldiers spent the morning searching in vain; they encountered only a few women and children. At noon, a group of men were instructed to break for lunch in a clearing by the log cabin. As they stacked their rifles, one fell and accidentally discharged. Unknown to the soldiers, there were scores of Indians hiding in the woods around the clearing. One or more of the Indians apparently assumed they had been discovered and returned fire. The soldiers took refuge in the cabin and continued the battle. By the time the Indians retreated into the oblivion of the forest, six soldiers lay dead, including Major Wilkinson (for whom the tiny village near Leech Lake on Highway 371 is named), and ten were wounded. The Indians apparently suffered no casualties although it was rumored that one had been killed. It is to the credit of the military that vengeance was not taken. "Old Bug" was allowed to make good his escape to the cabin of his brother, Chief Red Blanket, on Boy River, and peace was restored. When the citizens of the tiny village of Walker heard the shots from Sugar Point and when no one returned from the fighting to report its outcome, they feared the worst and assumed that the Indians had wiped out the military expedition. They called the Mayor of Brainerd and asked that he organize what amounted to a citizen's militia to help them. Mayor Nevers responsded and a special train left Brainerd for Walker. Dr. James Camp[1] was among those who volunteered.

Pauline Wold,[2] who worked for Dr. Camp, wrote the following account of Brainerd's reaction to the uprising:

"Leech Lake was only sixty miles away, and Indians on the warpath might easily reach us! And with all our men and guns gone, we felt very much like 'babes in the woods.'"

"Few people in Brainerd slept much that night. The next day we tried to get into communication with Walker, but the wires had evidently been cut, and no trains were running. The second day wild rumors were abroad that Indians on their ponies had rushed through town, but there was no news from Walker. On the morning of the third day Mrs. Nevers[3] called to find out if we had heard anything at the hospital, but we had not. She said she had heard that there had been a battle and that several men from Brainerd had been injured or killed, among them, Dr. Camp. Not very good news for us! We were all feeling pretty "jittery." On the following morning a wire reached the hospital asking us to meet a train coming down that morning, and to bring

[1]Dr. Camp was a highly respected and well-liked pioneer physician in Brainerd. He also owned a cabin near the thoroughfare between the Upper and Lower Mission Lakes. A "pothole" between the lakes and the Mississippi River is named for him. The author's father recalled that the doctor's well-trained horse would allow Camp to shoot partridges and other game from the buggy and would patiently wait while he retrieved them or gave chase.

[2]Wold, Pauline, Some recollections of the Leech Lake Uprising, Minnesota History, 1943.

[3]The wife of the Mayor of Brainerd.

Troops arrive in Walker, October, 1898.

A cabin and garden belonging to "Old Chief Bug"—the setting for the last Indian-White war.

soup, hot coffee, and surgical dressings. I must admit we were rather an excited crowd at the station. With sinking hearts we noticed as the train pulled in that there were several rough pine boxes in the baggage car. A shudder went through me when I thought that perhaps Dr. Camp was in one of them! Imagine our relief when the first to get off the train were Dr. Camp and Mayor Nevers. They told us at once that all the men from Brainerd were safe.

"Not many questions were asked, as soon we were busy feeding and dressing wounded soldiers and trying to make them a little more comfortable for a trip down to Fort Snelling hospital. They told us that half a dozen soldiers had been killed, among them the beloved Major Melville C. Wilkinson, and that ten had been wounded. One of the boys had been shot through the thigh. They were indignant to think that some of them had gone through the Cuban campaign without a scratch, and here they were being killed by a handful of Indians.

Courtesy of the Minnesota Historical Society

The village of Cass Lake was worried, too. This fortification was still standing two or three years after the battle when this picture was taken.

"That evening we had a little party to welcome Dr. Camp. A few neighbors came in, and we then heard from him what had really happened. Upon reaching Walker, the Brainerd men found everything in great commotion and everyone scared to death. They heard that the soldiers, eighty of them under the command of General John M. Bacon and Major Wilkinson, had gone to Sugar Point near Bear Island in the morning, as news had reached them that 'Old Bug' had been seen there. At Walker a lot of shooting had been heard during the day, but no one had returned to tell what was happening. It was feared that the Indians were getting the best of it.

"As Dr. Camp had spent a couple of years as the resident physician at Fort Totten, the men elected him their leader, thinking that perhaps he knew more about handling

Courtesy of the Minnesota Historical Society

Chief Flat Mouth, the younger. His refusal to support "Old Bug" helped spell doom for the Indian revolt.

Steam Hauler pulling loads of logs around the turn of the century.

Courtesy of Cass County Historical Society

Logging railroad, Cuba Hill area. This may be the trail now used as the Sucker Bay road which passes the Cuba Hill forestry tower.

Indians than they did. So the first thing he did was to gather all the women and children into the Walker Hotel, the only brick building in town. Next he placed guards on all the roads leading into town. 'I knew this was a very foolish precaution,' said Dr. Camp, 'for if the Indians wanted to come they would use their own trails that nobody else knew, and they would not use the beaten highways. But I did this to let people know that something was being done. I thought it might act as a nerve sedative - something they needed very badly just then.'

"The Brainerd group talked things over during the night and decided to cross the lake as soon as daybreak came and find out what was happening. Early the next morning they got a large barge and also some cordwood, which they piled in the center as a barricade to hide behind in case of need.

"At the 'Narrows' before entering the big lake, the party found a band of Indians, headed by Chief Flatmouth.[1] They called and asked, 'Where are you going?' The men answered, 'Over to Sugar Point to see what is happening over there,' and the Indians replied, 'We will be here when you come back.'

"When the barge neared the point, the men went ahead very cautiously, not knowing what might be coming. Everything seemed very quiet, with only a few men running down to the beach. They seemed to be in soldiers' uniforms, but that could be a disguise and they might be Indians. The newcomers beached their boat very carefully and went behind the barricade in case they should be shot at. To their relief, however, they were greeted by soldiers and a couple of newspaper reporters who had gone along to write up the happenings at Leech Lake. A couple of more frightened men were never seen. They climbed aboard like two little monkeys and swiftly hid behind the barricade.'

"Of course, by this time the action was over and the reporters had nothing to fear."

And so ended the last of the "Indian Wars!"
.

LOGGING

The lumber industry in this area is synonymous with the name of Thomas Barlow Walker - whose name is preserved through the community he founded on the western shores of Leech Lake and the Walker Art Gallerys of Minneapolis. Born in Xenia, Ohio, in 1840, young Walker came to Minneapolis at twenty-two years of age. At nineteen, he had contracted for railroad ties at Paris, Illinois; next, he tried teaching; but his first employment in Minnesota was as a surveyor for the St. Paul and Duluth Railroads. By 1868 he was owner of an extensive acreage of pine forests. One of his early mills was at Crookston. In his years at Walker and in the Leech Lake area he was associated with a number of lumbermen, but the most significant of these associations was with Henry Akeley. For him he named the townsite where he constructed one of his largest mills when he became disgusted with the number of saloons in Walker. There was much consternation among the Walker businessmen when he announced his decision to build his new mill ten miles to the west, but he could not be dissuaded. The original deeds for property in Akeley included the prohibition of liquor traffic. The Akeley of today is much smaller than the original lumbering "boom town."

The upper reaches of the Crow Wing and several of the lakes through which the river winds were logged-off by Walker and Akeley and in 1898 the partnership constructed a mill in that area.

[1]Chief Flatmouth II, son of the legendary Chief of the Pillagers of the first part of the century. Apparently there were many Indians who wanted no part of the uprising, nor did "Old Bug" have the affection or respect of all Leech Lake Indians.

But much of the region could not be harvested effectively without railroads; and thus it was logging that provided the original impetus for the construction of a network of railroads in Northern Minnesota around the turn of the century:

Brainerd, Walker, and Bemidji were connected by the Brainerd and Northern Minnesota Railway. It reached Walker in 1896 and was extended to Bemidji in 1897-99. In 1901 it was purchased by the Minnesota and International Railway - with offices in Brainerd.

Park Rapids and Cass Lake were connected by the Park Rapids and Leech Lake Railway in 1899. This line was purchased by the Great Northern in 1907.

Federal Dam, Cass Lake, Bemidji, and Plummer were connected in 1909 with an extension (east to west) of the Canadian based Minneapolis, St. Paul, and Sault St. Marie Railroad (Soo Line).

The Great Northern also crossed this area from east to west through the village of Cass Lake.

All Existing railroads in the area are now a part of the Burlington Northern system.

Minnesota timber and iron have built much of central United States. Homes, schools, churches, factories, railroads, office buildings and construction of all kinds came from these two great Minnesota resources. But the supposedly endless supply of trees was really quite limited after all and by World War I the lumbering boom was pretty well over. Between the two world wars most of the cutting was used for pulp for the manufacture of paper; this was second growth poplar and jack pine. Today we are seeing a revival of the lumbering industry; this time with much better management.

Much of the Leech Lake area is now a part of the Chippewa National Forest where logging is closely supervised by the U.S. Forest Service. The forest was established in 1902 by an Act of Congress during the administration of Theodore Roosevelt. It was named the Minnesota National Forest in 1908, but the name was changed to "Chippewa" in 1928. Good forest management not only provides for a harvest of timber, but also improves the habitat for all kinds of wildlife. Virgin pine forests are

Courtesy of the Minnesota Historical Society

This is believed to be the first photograph of the village of Walker—taken about 1896.

beautiful and even inspirational to behold, but they form an umbrella which screens out life-giving sunlight and eliminates the undergrowth which provides food for both birds and animals.

During the 1930's when the legends of Paul Bunyan were revived, the Leech Lake Indians recalled a legend of their own. They told how their folk hero - Nanabozho - saved the Leech-Cass Lake area from complete devastation by Paul Bunyan. Just when it seemed white man would not be satisfied until every tree was gone, Nanabozho appeared in response to Pillager prayers. The great Indian took on Paul Bunyan in a battle of giants. Almost as much timber was destroyed where the two fought and wrestled as by the axe. Finally the stalemate was broken when Nanabozho picked up a frozen eelpout and struck Paul a sickening blow "across the chops." Defeated, Paul Bunyan sulked off to Brainerd, where, in ignorance, white man accepted him as a hero before he ruined that area as well.

Courtesy of the Minnesota Historical Society

The beginning of a new era: recreation. This well-dressed fishing party apparently used bamboo poles to catch all these walleyes, northerns, bass, and suckers in Leech Lake in 1896.

ALL GOOD HUNTING AND FISHING IS NOT IN THE PAST

Harry Wolf, Curt Kiffmeyer, and Jim Kiffmeyer with November bluebills.

Bruce Lund shows off his baking-size Northern.

Steve Clabots with trophy-size winter Walleye and Northern.

Jerry Hayenga harpooned this twenty-one pounder at the mouth of Sucker Bay.

These youthful master-fishermen are (left to right) Randy Card, Jeff Dravis, Darrell Card, Blaine Dravis, Lynnell Card, and Greg Dravis.

A Staples High School Champion Wrestling Team prove they are also champion fishermen. Left to right: Doug Shequen, Steve O'Keefe, Doug Roberts, Jerry Stone, Tony Van Buren, Jerry Rengel, Dave Roberts, Dave Sowers, Dave Sikora, and Jeff Cizek.

Winter or Summer — Leech Lake still produces great walleye fishing.

Neil Krough spreads the wings of his Greater Canada Goose.

Jerry Hayenga adds a two-year old black bear to this "hanging tree" on Sucker Bay.

The author and his 224 pound, Leech Lake buck.

Greg Hayenga poses with his Sucker Bay "fork" buck.

CHAPTER THREE
The Crow Wing River

Historic water highway - gateway for the Indian to the central lake region - legendary hunting ground - carrier of mammoth white pine logs at the turn of the century - sanctuary of walleye pike and northerns - popular present day canoe trail - clear as a mountain stream in summer - heavily forested in pine and birch - what a river!

Why the name Crow Wing?

Tradition tells us that the river received its name from the wing-shaped island at its mouth; others say it was so named because this same island was the headquarters of Chief Crow - ancestor to the "Little Crows" of the Sioux tribe.

According to some early white settlers, the river is named for an Indian maiden whose name was "Crow Wing." She is supposedly remembered because she took her own life by drowning in the river in preference to her father's choice of a husband for her.

The Sioux simply called it "Pine River."

Jonathan Carver, the Massachusetts-born explorer of the Minnesota River Valley in the 1760's, produced a map of the Minnesota area, but everything north of Rum River was by hearsay. On his map, the "Marshy River" and the "Lake River" were probably the Long Prairie and the Crow Wing.

Relatively speaking, we really know very little of the full history of this great stream and its tributaries; the Gull, Long Prairie, Partridge, Leaf, and Shell Rivers. For several thousands of years man used these streams as his best means of travel across what is now Central Minnesota. We know practically nothing of what happened before the 1700's. Our tales of the river go back, therefore, only a little more than two hundred years. It is exciting, however, to think of the prehistoric Crow Wing as an ancient setting for a drama of human history - featuring real people - century after century after century. These were human beings with the same basic desires, needs, and emotions as you and I. They loved, hated, fought, worked, hunted, fished, played, planned, dreamed, mourned, rejoiced, worshipped . . .

We enjoy the Crow Wing, but it was important to their survival!

THE BATTLE AT THE MOUTH OF THE CROW WING RIVER[1]

Perhaps it would be well to begin our story by finishing a tale we began in our chapter about Leech Lake.

It was in 1768 - just a little more than two hundred years ago - there were rumblings of revolt among the European colonists along our eastern seaboard. It had been about thirty years since the Sioux were driven from their strongholds throughout the lake region, but they had contended on even terms with the Ojibway for all of these years for control of the woodlands of Minnesota. It had not been until only two years earlier, in 1766, that the Dakotas finally suffered a decisive defeat at the hands of the Ojibway, a defeat from which they would never really recover. But they refused to accept the Ojibway victory as final and invaded the lake region again and again for nearly one hundred years.

You will recall from our tales of Leech Lake, that this was the occasion on which the Dakotas had launched a major attack from their headquarters village at the mouth of the Rum River against the new capital of the Ojibway at Sandy Lake. It was really a small army of about two hundred braves. At about the same time, the Ojibway sent a

[1]Although this account comes from several sources, William Warren's version is the one most often quoted.

war party of about seventy men south down the Mississippi with the Rum River village as their objective. The Dakotas proceeded up the Mississippi, but chose to take the Crow Wing cutoff, then traveled up the Gull River; across Gull, Long, and Whitefish Lakes; then up to Pine River and across a series of lakes leading to Boy River and then Leech Lake - on the way to Sandy Lake (probably because there was less current to fight). Thus the two war parties did not meet on their way to their respective objectives.

Apparently the Ojibways did not find any indication that the Sioux army had traveled up the river only days before. They were evidently totally surprised to find the Rum River village deserted, with the women and children safely protected elsewhere. Surprise turned to horror when the Ojibways realized the possible significance of the empty village. Their worst fears were to be realized. The Dakotas had fallen on the helpless Sandy Lake village and slaughtered everyone except thirty young women whom they took captive along with an older woman to care for them. The Ojibway wasted no time looking for the hidden Dakota women and children but hurried back up river - intent on finding a battlefield of their liking to ambush the Sioux. They reached the mouth of the Crow Wing without encountering the enemy, and here they finally discovered camp signs left by the Dakotas on their way north. They dared go no further because they were not sure by which river the Sioux would come - the Crow Wing or the Mississippi. They quickly dug in on a bluff on the east bank of the Mississippi, overlooking both rivers (where their excavations may be seen to this day as a part of Crow Wing State Park). They did not have long to wait. A scout reported that the Sioux war party was on its way down the Mississippi. They stopped across from Crow Wing Island, where they forced their captives to serve them breakfast, in full view of their loved ones who were anxiously lying in ambush.

As the story goes, the old woman whose life had been spared to care for the captives turned out to be the real heroine. She had quietly reminded her charges that there was a good chance they would meet the returning men from their village somewhere along the river. If and when this should happen, she urged the women to overturn their canoes and swim towards the rifle fire. And that is exactly what happened. The unsuspecting Dakotas were caught completely off guard and suffered heavy casualties. The Ojibway had chosen their battleground well. Here the Mississippi narrowed and made a sharp turn, the faster current bringing the Sioux into close range. But they were not about to give up their captives or leave without a good fight. Incensed over the sudden turn of events and the fact they had been outsmarted by their captives - women at that (the Indians were real male chauvinists!) - they placed the Ojibway under siege. When frontal attacks proved too costly, they crossed the river and circled behind them on land. But the Ojibway were too well protected and continued to get the better of the battle. At last, the Dakotas decided "discretion was indeed the better part of valor" and reluctantly turned their canoes down stream - no doubt keenly disappointed at their loss of the captives and many of their own men, and perhaps wondering about the safety of their families they had left behind - hopefully secluded and protected.

As in all wars, everyone lost something, and in this case, no one gained anything.

AN INCIDENT AT PILLAGER CREEK

We shall not retell the tale of the party of Leech Lake Ojibways who, in 1781, came across the dying trader and his voyageurs and confiscated his goods and how this event may have precipitated the spread of the smallpox plague - but we would remind you that the Crow Wing River - at the mouth of Pillager Creek - was the setting for this significant bit of history.

And it was from this incident, many believe, that the creek, the tribe, and the city on the banks of the Crow Wing all received the name "Pillager" - describing those who pillage or take by force.[1]

DAKOTAS ATTACK A FRENCH TRADING POST AT THE MOUTH OF THE PARTRIDGE

This tale is from the lips of none other than Chief Flat Mouth (the elder) of the Leech Lake Pillagers - and was told first hand to William Warren, the Ojibway historian.

One winter, when Flat Mouth was a child and too young to bear arms (around 1780), he accompanied members of his tribe to the confluence of the Partridge (or Pena River) and the Crow Wing, where a French Trader had constructed a post only that fall. The Ojibway called the trader "Ah-wish-to-yah," which meant "Blacksmith." Several voyageurs were there with him at the time and together with the Pillager hunters and trappers totalled about forty men working out of the post. Most of the Indians had brought their families with them, even though they knew there was a good chance of an encounter with Dakota hunters or even war parties. The trader was also aware of the danger, but a heavy population of beaver had drawn him there.

Expecting the worst, the men erected a log barricade around the post and the wigwams.

Late one night, ten of the Pillager hunters awakened those at the post with the alarming news that a sizable band of Dakotas were in the area. They had crossed their trail and identified them by the lingering smell of tobacco (which was distinctly different from the ground inner-bark of the kinnikinic smoked by the Ojibways). The Sioux were following a trail which would lead them to a small, defenseless camp of Pillager hunters. Craftily, the Ojibways circled ahead of the Sioux and crossed the trail, hoping to lure them to the more easily defended barricade at the trading post. The strategy worked. By the time the Sioux arrived, the barricade had been strengthened and nearly twenty men (French and Ojibway) were ready for the attack.

The party of Dakotas was large indeed - about two hundred braves - but whereas the men at the post were all armed with guns, the Sioux were forced to depend on bows and arrows and had only a half-dozen rifles among them.

The huge war party finally appeared on the bank across from the trading post. Confident in their numerical superiority, they leisurely put on their paint, feathers, and other ornaments. Then, sounding their war whoops, they charged across the ice sending a cloud of arrows into the fortification. But the defenders were well protected and their rifle fire was devastating. No Dakota warrior reached the barricade. With a change in strategy, the Sioux began firing their arrows almost straight up, lobbing them - like mortar fire - into the compound. The shower of barbed missiles was more effective and two Ojibway hunters were wounded seriously enough to take them out of action. Some took refuge in the post itself. But in the end, the rifles proved to be more than an equalizing factor and a frustrated Sioux war party - with a greatly diminished supply of arrows - finally recognized the futility of the situation.

[1]Others believe the Leech Lake Ojibway were called "Pillagers" prior to this event and merely gave their name to the location by what they did there.

Before leaving, they cut holes in the river ice and gave their dead a watery burial. Shortly after their departure, other hunters and trappers who had heard the shooting arrived at the post - about twenty reinforcements in all. Realizing that the Dakotas were nearly out of arrows, they wanted to press their advantage by pursuing them. The Trader argued to the contrary and finally prevailed.

It is interesting that at this date, about 1780, the Dakotas had so few guns. It may have been that they came from the western prairies and had, therefore, little opportunity to procure them.

CADOTTE WINTERS AT THE MOUTH OF THE LEAF RIVER[1]

John Baptiste Cadotte, more than anyone else, opened the Minnesota lake region to the Northwest Company fur traders. Following his graduation from college in Montreal, he received a legacy of 40,000 francs from his father.[2] With this capital he entered into the trading business.

In 1792 he organized a large expedition for the purpose of exploring the sources of the Mississippi River and carrying on trade as he went. Actually, he divided his expedition into several contingents. The group under his leadership proceeded down the Mississippi, up the Crow Wing, and then, because of all the beaver sign, decided to winter at the mouth of the Leaf River. Other units wintered at Prairie Portage on the Red River and at Pembina.

The Pillagers, weary of their limitations on the islands of Leech Lake and dissatisfied with the poor winter hunting, believed they would be relatively safe in the company of the Whites and followed along - hunting and trapping for furs to trade and for meat for survival.

A number of women were included in the Cadotte expedition, but because he was heading into Sioux territory, most of them were left at Fond du Lac for the winter.

At the mouth of the Leaf, Cadotte and his crew erected several log cabins and surrounded them with a stockade. Hunting was good, and a winter's supply of buffalo, elk, bear, and deer were soon in store. Once the camp was secure, Cadotte sent most of his men out in small bands to trap and hunt - especially for beaver.

Early one morning a large party of Sioux appeared in battle dress. With war whoops they advanced on the stockade, and once in range, showered it with arrows and discharged the few guns in their possession. (further indication that the Sioux had less opportunity than the Ojibway to trade with the Whites.) Even though two of his men had been wounded, Cadotte ordered them not to shoot. Instead he raised the British "Union Jack" for identification and a white flag to indicate he wanted to talk.

The Indians ceased their attack, and after a brief consultation, a number of braves approached the gate. Cadotte stood in the opening and spoke through his enterpreter, a man named Rasle. He told them that he had not come to wage war, but to trade. The Dakotas accepted this explanation and replied that they had thought they were a band of Ojibway, come to exploit their best hunting grounds. They offered to smoke the pipe of peace. Cadotte invited the chief and other leaders into his cabin, while his men kept an anxious eye on the Sioux who remained outside.

Cadotte gave the Indians presents of tobacco, meat, and ammunition. The Sioux,

---

[1]Most of this account is based on William Warren's "History of the Ojibway." The location at the mouth of the Leaf River has never been positively verified but is accepted by most.

[2]The senior Cadotte was a successful trader; in a single winter he and his colleagues took in about 12,000 beaver skins.

in return, insisted that he return with them to their village, about a day's travel away, where they said they had many beaver skins. Cadotte agreed. He took with him thirty of his best men; well armed, and carrying packs of trade items, they returned with the Dakotas to their village.

The camp proved to be a large one - over one hundred lodges. The Whites were well received and feasted on choice cuts of venison, elk, and bear. Cadotte was housed in the chief's own lodge, where he set himself up in business and traded with a continuous stream of Indians all that night. By morning he had all the beaver hides his men could carry. Unfortunately he had many trade items left over. This fact apparently upset the Dakotas who had few contacts with traders and did not want to see all these treasures leave their village. At any rate, they plotted an ambush on the return trip.

As Cadotte and his heavily laden voyageurs left the village, they were accompanied by the Chief and a number of warriors. Rasle, the interpreter, noted that there were no men in the village when they left that morning - just those who accompanied them. About half-way back to the stockade, just short of a heavily-wooded area, the chief indicated that he and his men wanted to rest and smoke awhile but that the Whites should go on ahead with their loads - and they would soon catch up. At this point, Rasle relayed his suspicions to Cadotte - suggesting that an ambush lay ahead in the grove of trees. The trader reacted quickly by placing the barrel of his revolver against the chest of the chief. Others disarmed the outnumbered warriors. When the chief realized that the truth was out, he wept for his life and the safety of his men. On Cadotte's orders, he sent one of his braves ahead and soon a small army of Sioux warriors filed out of the wooded area and headed back to the village. Cadotte took the chief and his men to the stockade as hostages until he could warn his men and the Pillagers that the Sioux could not be trusted and to be on guard. When he finally released the Dakotas, he again gave them presents - in the hope they would be willing to "let by-gones be by-gones" and enjoy a peaceful co-existence. It worked. The Dakotas were not seen again near the stockade or in the area where Cadotte's hunters and trappers were harvesting furs.

The trader's journal revealed a tale of tragedy in late winter - perhaps the result of "cabin fever." A voyageur named Bell was accompanied by a huge black servant called "Negro Tom." One night when both had been drinking heavily the two got into a fight and the black giant soon had Bell on the floor. The white man's Indian wife was present, and fearing for her husband's life, attacked Tom with a knife and killed him. The big bones of Negro Tom are buried in an unmarked grave near the mouth of the Leaf.

That spring, Cadotte's expedition broke camp and continued up the Leaf River. They eventually portaged into Ottertail Lake and from there worked their way west to the Red River and then downstream, North.

MINNESOTA'S BEST HUNTING GROUNDS?

The Crow Wing and its tributaries may have provided the best hunting of our state. Not only did it offer ideal habitat for all fur bearing animals, but there was ample cover and forage for deer and elk. Bear were also plentiful. In addition, it provided entry for the woodland Indians to the prairies with their enormous herds of buffalo.

William Warren reported that the famous Ojibway warrior and hunter, Noka,[1] for whom the Nokasippi was named, in one day - starting at the mouth of the Crow Wing - killed sixteen elk, four buffalo, five deer, three bear, one lynx and a porcupine! He gave them to a trader who was spending the winter at the village of Crow Wing as his supply of meat for the cold season. Now that's a hunting story!

These hunting grounds were so important to both the Sioux and the Ojibway that when neither was able to conclusively drive the other from it, a winter truce was negotiated several years running. Prior to this time, a hunter might very well return to his camp at night with a scalp or two hanging from his belt as well as furs taken during the day. The truce also made it possible to take the entire family on the winter hunt.

So good was the hunting that the Ojibway came from as far away as Leech and Sandy Lakes; these two tribes retained a close relationship over the years and it was their custom to rendezvous at Gull Lake or the mouth of the Crow Wing on their way to the winter hunting grounds. The virgin pine forests of the north were not good habitat for wildlife because insufficient light could filter through to nourish the undergrowth which provides food for both birds and animals. The Sioux came from as far away as the prairies of present day North and South Dakota, and included the Wahpetons and Sissetons as well as other Dakota bands.

The Ojibway bands often traveled up the Long Prairie River and camped in the vicinity of the city of the same name. They were especially attracted by the herds of buffalo that grazed in the area. The Sioux were usually there first and already settled in their hide-covered tepees. After warring back and forth all summer, the only way the Ojibway could be certain the winter truce would again be in effect was to directly approach the Sioux village and offer to smoke the pipe of peace. Dressed for the occasion and well armed, a vanguard - not so large as to be threatening but not so small as to be easy prey - would march right into the Sioux village. The bearer of the peace pipe and the banner carriers lead the procession. The customary response of the Sioux was to welcome the Ojibway with a volley of rifle fire. Sometimes the singing bullets were so near the ears of the visitors that it seemed the "name of the game" was to come as close as possible without scoring! Once it was clear that a truce was desired, the Ojibway were welcomed into the lodges of the Sioux where they smoked the peace pipe and feasted on the best available food - sometimes literally beneath the scalps of their fellow tribesmen which may have been taken as recently as the past summer and now hung suspended from the lodge poles. The Ojibway had a word for this ceremony; they called it "Pin-dig-u-daud-e-win," which is translated, "to enter into one another's lodges."

An interesting custom during these periods of truce was for warriors to adopt "brothers" from among the traditional enemies of the other tribes. Often they were considered as replacements for special friends or brothers lost in battle. There are many tales of adopted brothers being spared during massacres or scalping parties.

An exception is the story of Yellow Hair - father of Chief Flat Mouth. He and his family had lingered at Long Prairie after the Pillagers had moved down river on the way back to Leech Lake. He returned from his hunt one day to find his oldest son murdered and mutilated; he blamed the Sioux. After returning to Leech Lake to bury the body of his son, he organized a small group of warriors to help gain revenge. Fellow tribesmen who did not want the truce broken, tried in vain to dissuade him:

[1]This is the Noka of the 1700's, grandfather of Chief White Fisher.

Yellow Hair did not really know who murdered his son, but decided to follow the trail left by two lodges of the Sioux. So great was his hate that he stayed on the trail for about two hundred miles before gaining sight of them. He recognized one of the warriors as his adopted brother. Even so, he broke the taboo, and he and his men killed everyone in his "brother's" lodge - even though he could not be certain he was guilty. The second lodge was well defended, so Yellow Hair, his revenge satisfied, returned to Leech Lake.

COMING OF THE WHITES

Although temporary or "winter" trading posts were established on the Crow Wing at the mouth of the Partridge and the Leaf Rivers, the only "permanent" post was at the mouth of the Crow Wing itself. Although there may also have been "winter posts" here as early as the days when the Sioux controlled the area, the first permanent post was established in 1837 by Clem Beaulieu.

Except for the traders, white settlers were not legally allowed in Minnesota until after the Chippewa and Sioux treaties of 1837 were ratified.

In 1847, Fort Ripley was constructed on the Mississippi near the mouth of the Crow Wing to encourage settlement and to enforce peace betwen the Ojibway and the Sioux.

The village of Crow Wing began as a frontier trading center and Father Pierz established one of his many mission stations here. The "Chippewa Agency" was established nearby in 1852, on the Crow Wing a short distance from the mouth of the Gull River. It was actually transferred here from Sandy Lake. It was discontinued when the Ojibway were moved to White Earth in 1868.

The Winnebago Agency was at Long Prairie.

In the 1850's, a military road was constructed along the east bank of the Mississippi to Crow Wing; this was a strong inducement to the settling of the area.

THE OLD CROW WING TRAIL

In the 1800's, as the White settlements grew at the Canadian outpost of Pembina and Selkirk, strong ties were developed with Minneapolis and St. Paul; too much wilderness stood between the Red River and Montreal.[1] Three major trails were developed between the Pembina-Red River area and St. Paul:[2] one led south on the west side of the Red River and then southwest along the Minnesota River; a second followed on the east side of the Red River and then circumvented the woodlands - crossing the prairies to St. Cloud; a third was the Crow Wing Trail.

Starting at Pembina, the trail followed the north-south gravel ridges of the ancient shores of Lake Agassiz; then, after crossing the Sand Hill River, as the gravel ridges turned too much in an easterly direction to be followed, a high, dry prairie route was taken to the Red Lake River and on to the Wild Rice River; here the terrain changed to one of hills and small lakes; after reaching Detroit Lake, the trail followed the shoreline; from here it lead among patches of heavy woods (oak, elm, basswood, etc.) to Rush Lake, the Ottertail River, and then Ottertail Lake; from here the trail

[1]The Canadian government was very much concerned with these ties between their settlers and the twin cities and developed the Dawson Trail from the Northwest Angle of the Lake of the Woods west to Fort Garry (present site of Winnipeg).

[2]Although Canadians traveled to St. Paul by ox cart in the 1820's, the trails received their greatest use in the 1880's.

followed the Leaf River to the Crow Wing (some sort of over-night inn and other buildings were once located here on the west bank of the Crow Wing; the site is now called "Old Wadena"[1]) after crossing the Crow Wing, the trail followed the east bank of the Crow Wing River to the village of Crow Wing.[2]

All sorts of animal drawn vehicles were used on the trails, but most of them were the legendary oxcarts. Oxen proved more durable and sure-footed than horses in crossing the many boggy and swampy areas, even though most were spanned by corduroy roads.[3] The carts themselves were mostly two-wheelers. The squeal of wood on wood as the huge wooden wheels turned on wooden axels could be heard for miles. For the most part, they carried buffalo hides, buffalo tongues, pemmican, and furs south and manufactured goods and supplies north.

In the 1820's, more than three hundred disillusioned Swiss settlers of the Selkirk colony moved down the trails to Fort Snelling[4] - carrying their possessions in oxcarts and driving their livestock before them.

Oxcart traffic increased until it was estimated that in the late 1850's, some five to six hundred carts were using the trails between St. Paul and Pembina each year. The length of time the journey would take varied according to the time of year, weather conditions, the equipment, the driver, etc. But to make the journey in three weeks one had to be moving right along.

In 1858, the St. Paul Chamber of Commerce offered $10,000 to the first man to put a steamboat on the Red River. Anson Northup responded by sailing a steamer up the Mississippi to Crow Wing. There he dismantled the ship and then used thirty-four teams of oxen to transport it across country that winter to the Red River - where it was reassembled and won the promised reward for its owner.

When the Sioux were on the warpath or during periods of high danger of prairie fires, the Crow Wing Trail became the most popular of the three routes.

LOGGING

The first major industry in the history of Minnesota was fur trading; the second was logging. The Crow Wing River and its tributaries were a center for both.

The Sioux had called the Crow Wing "the Pine River." It was well-named. Giant white pine - and some Norways - lined its banks and spread out over thousands of acres of higher ground in all directions. The jack pine, seen everywhere in the region today was much less plentiful in the days of the virgin forests.

Lumbering had its beginning in Minnesota following the Indian Treaties of 1837 in the triangle between the St. Croix and the Mississippi Rivers. It reached the Crow Wing area just ten years later (1847); nearly half a century before the Leech Lake area had its logging boom. An agreement was reached with Chief Hole-in-the-Day (the elder) of Gull Lake and a logging camp was set up near the mouth of the River. A million and a half feet of logs were cut the first year and sent down stream (1847-48).

Many names are associated with the logging of the Crow Wing watershed, but none remain as familiar to us as that of Frederick Weyerhaueser, German-born lumber baron. Founded in Illinois in 1860, his company moved its influence steadily

---

[1]"Wadena" is Ojibway for "little round hill." There was also a second crossing a little further upstream. A townsite was registered here by Augustus Aspinwall with the name "Wadena." Some maintain that as many as 100 people lived here about 1855. A North West Co. Trading Post is believed to have been located here on the West bank of the Crow Wing about 1790.

[2]Shultz, Sir John Christian, The Old Crow Wing Trail, Manitoba Free Press, 1894.

[3]A road made of logs laid side by side in the mud.

[4]According to the famous Indian Agent at Fort Snelling, Lawrence Taliaferro, about 330 of the colonists had appeared at the fort by the fall of 1827.

The above documents indicate that many Motley citizens were concerned about an Indian uprising in 1884. Their petition for help was sent to Governor Hubbard.

Courtesy of Ed Morey

Logs destined for the Crow Wing—and then to help build America.   Photo courtesy Ed Morey

northward and included this area when it purchased the Pine Tree Company of Little Falls and then, in cooperation with other lumber groups, purchased huge land holdings from the Northern Pacific Railroad. Today the Weyerhaueser enterprises extend to the west coast.

There was much cooperation - and sometimes collusion - among the lumber magnates. Sometimes legal partnerships were organized, other times there were negotiations behind the scenes such as in the bidding on timber on Indian lands.

Many names are remembered from these years, including Walker, Backus, Akeley, Shevlin, Pillsbury and others. Some operators were not so big but are remembered because they gave their names to communities or townships or other landmarks. King Staples, for example, logged the area where a city now bears his name - from 1878 to 1881. In later years the Dower Lumber Company operated in the same region and a little lake west of Staples is called "Dower Lake" until this day.

The Wilson Brothers, George and William, of Park Papids, were among the names associated with the logging of the Crow Wing and its tributaries. They are good examples of the "middle management" of that day. They often worked for or were financed by the lumber magnates and in turn actually planned the cutting and hired the men. In George Wilson's memoirs, as recorded by Charles Vandersluis of Bemidji, he tells of:

John Moberg operating on the Shell River in the 1880's;

The Wilson brothers supervising the cutting and sending of forty or fifty million feet of logs down the river in 1893 from the sixth, seventh, and eighth Crow Wing Lakes - they all were marked for Akeley and sent to his Minneapolis mill;

Jerry Howe's operation on the Eighth Crow Wing Lake in 1898, with all logs being sold in Minneapolis;

SAW MILL OPERATIONS AT MOTLEY AT THE TURN OF THE CENTURY

The barrells on top of the building are filled with water for use in case of fire.

All photos courtesy Ed Morey

The construction of the Walker-Akeley mill on the Upper Crow Wing in 1898;

The Wilson's operation on Eighth Crow Wing during the winters of 1899 to 1901 where they built a dam at the outlet;[1] *and*

The operations of Carpenter and Lamb in 1905.

Once the logs reached the Mississippi they were usually handled by the Mississippi and Rum River Boom Company on their way to Minneapolis or dropped off at mills along the way. Logs were all registered to their owners in the Surveyor General's office - they were branded much as cattle (a special mallet was used with a design in the head).

H.B. Morrison had a saw mill operation at Motley from the 1880's into this century, making that community one of the busiest lumbering centers of that day. Morrison also manufactured bricks.

Wanigans[2] were used on all of the Crow Wing Lakes and on the river as well. In high water, paddlewheel steamboats[3] ventured up both the Crow Wing and the Long Prairie Rivers. After the railroad came to Motley, grain was hauled from Long Prairie down the river on barges to that community.

The Gull River had a unique logging history all its own and this is discussed in our tales of Gull Lake.

Lumbering remains an important industry in the Crow Wing basin and in more recent years has been dominated by the Park Region Timber Company and the Northwest Paper Company[4] of Brainerd. Yet, many individuals still earn a living for themselves and their families by cutting timber of pulpwood (for paper) independently or in small partnerships.

The lumberjacks of old were a singing people, and during the peak years the industry was glamorized by a number of ballads, including "The Crow Wing Drive."

Says White Pine Tom to Arkansaw

"There's one more drive that I'd like to strike."

Says Arkansaw, "What can it be? "

"It's the Crow Wing River for the Old Pine Tree."

THE CROW WING RIVER TODAY

This magnificant stream with its history of Indian wars, trapping, trading, and logging - today offers one of the finest canoe trails in our state. The river moves at a moderately rapid pace - about four miles per hour - and has a summer depth of from one and one-half to six feet. The stream is remarkably safe in that it can be waded most everywhere and the deep water is found in relatively small holes or channels. The deeper water provides good fishing - particularly in spring and fall. There are many rapids, but usually only in shallow areas. The scenery is still beautiful, even though the pines are mostly gone. The quiet canoeist is frequently treated to sightings of wild animals and birds, especially migratory waterfowl. The stream has a genuine wilderness feeling even though one is always close to civilization. Farms and other evidences of civilization are surprisingly scarce because much of the surrounding area is flooded each spring.

[1] Over the years, a number of wooden dams were constructed between the Crow Wing Lakes (including a Weyerhauser dam at the outlet of first Crow Wing) and on the river itself to store water for the big drives; the river was normally too low to float the logs. One such dam was between McGivern Park and the Staples golf course.

[2] Wanigans were shacks built on flat boats. Some were used as kitchens, others as bunk houses.

[3] The steamer "Lotta Lee" was launched at Shell City on the Shell River in 1884. It eventually ran aground on the Crow Wing and was abandoned.

[4] A subsidiary of the Potlatch Corporation.

The official canoe trail begins at Blueberry Lake on the Shell River and ends at McGivern Park near Staples.

The following description of campsites is taken from a brochure published by the Crow Wing Canoe Trails Association:

The organized canoe trail begins at the Blueberry Bridge northeast of Menahga. From here, 13 campsites are spaced at convenient intervals, with no dams or portages to obstruct your trip. No hardships here, but a quiet, restful trip that even the small children will delight in, and the avid canoeist will appreciate. At each site there are toilet facilities, pumps and ample campgrounds. While you are on the river, supplies can be purchased at **Huntersville, Nimrod, Oylen and Wahoo Valley,** and telephone calls can be made at these points also.

The Wadena County Crow Wing Canoe Trail is varied and interesting. You don't need a guide and there are no charging rapids or windswept areas. The average current is 4 m.p.h. so an average canoeist will travel 20 to 30 miles a day. You may start or end your trip where you choose and you're never too far from settled area. In case of emergency, help is never far away.

SHELL CITY CAMPSITE — once the location of a flourishing factory making buttons from the shells of fresh water clams dug from the Shell River. 6 miles to

TREE FARM LANDING CAMPSITE — formerly a part of the surrounding Northwest Paper Company tree farm. This tree farm is managed for the production of perpetual crops of pulp wood and is open to the public for recreational pursuits. 3.5 miles to

HUNTERSVILLE TOWNSHIP CAMPSITE — is owned by the Huntersville Township board. For public recreation. .75 mile to

BIG BEND CAMPSITE — accessible by river only. 2.75 miles to

HUNTERSVILLE FOREST CAMPSITE — in the heart of the Huntersville State Forest, with miles of old logging trails - interesting hiking midst the pines. 7 miles to

ANDERSON'S CROSSING CAMPSITE — named for a pioneer settler, this Indian crossing is the beginning of the Butterfield Rapids. You will enjoy hiking the trails leading from this site. 5 miles to

STIGMAN'S MOUND CAMPSITE — at the Nimrod Bridge, established by the Nimrod Grange and named for former major league pitcher, Dick Stigman, whose home was Nimrod. 1 mile to

FRAME'S LANDING CAMPSITE — named for one of Nimrod's first citizen's. A CCC Camp was operated here in early 1940's. 2 miles to

INDIAN MOUNDS — these pre-historic Indian Mounds are accessible by canoe or automobile. Camping, campfires and picnicking are not permitted at this site. 4 miles to

LITTLE WHITE DOG CAMPSITE — an Indian lookout point with a beautiful view of the river. The high banks above this site were used for Indian ceremonies. Here sacrificial animals were killed honoring the Indian dieties. 5.5 miles to

KNOB HILL CAMPSITE — set on a picturesque Jack-pine flat. Fire damage south of this site reminds you to be careful with your campfires. 3 miles to

COTTINGHAM PARK CAMPSITE — a popular picnicking and swimming spot. Enjoy a nature hike on the trail leading south from the park. 5.5 miles to

BULLARD BLUFF CAMPSITE — known as Hog Haven in early Wadena County history because of the hogs running free. 4 miles to

OLD WADENA CAMPSITE — between the mouth of the Leaf and Partridge Rivers is the Old Wadena Historic Site. The name 'Wadena' is from the Chippewa word meaning 'little round hill.' 1.5 miles to

McGIVERN PARK CAMPSITE — is the end of the organized Wadena County Crow Wing Canoe Trail.

From First Crow Wing Lake to its confluence with the Mississippi, the river is eighty-seven miles long - and is completely unobstructed except for the two dams (Pillager and Sylvan) near its mouth.

The Minnesota Department of Natural Resources reports thirty-five species of fish and minnows in the stream with suckers and redhorse being the most common. Rock Bass is the most common variety of game fish - although not considered desirable by many fishermen. The DNR reports, however, that the Crow Wing rock bass are virtually parasite - free and probably deserve more attention from the sportsman. Other game fish found in the stream include large numbers of walleye and northern pike with concentrations of crappies, largemouth bass, and sunfish in the reservoirs behind the dams. Smallmouth bass are found in the lower four miles of the river below the Sylvan Dam. Among the rough fish the department lists dogfish, bullheads, perch, and burbot (eelpout). The DNR is considering the stocking of smallmouth bass in the upper river and catfish in the lower part of the stream.

"Old timers" have many stories of giant northerns and even muskies inhabiting the river; actually, a few old mounted muskellunge trophies are still around as supporting evidence. They probably came up the stream from the Mississippi before the construction of the dams.

A 1967 report to the Department of Natural Resources by Merle W. Johnson, Aquatic Biologist, suggests the feasibility of a dam at the foot of Webster's Rapids one mile above Nimrod, for the purpose of keeping carp out of the upper river and Crow Wing Lakes (this fish is now common in the Long Prairie River), and to provide an impoundment or small lake for about 4,500 feet upstream.

Excellent spawning areas are in abundance but the newly hatched "fry" are often trapped when the high water recedes in summer.

The clear, unpolluted waters of the magnificant Crow Wing River are surely one of the most valuable natural resources of our state. It is not hard to understand why so much Indian blood was shed for the right to control it.

Mike Matanich hooked all three of these ten pound walleyes in the Crow Wing River.

Photo courtesy L.J. "Pat" Miller

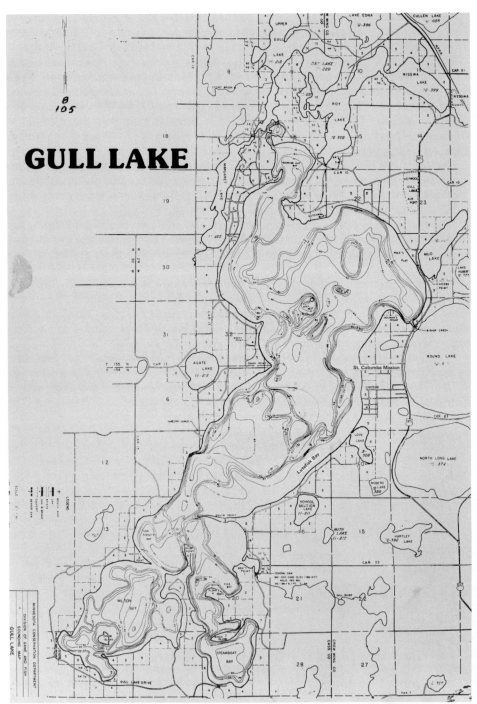

Courtesy of the Minnesota Department of Natural Resources

CHAPTER FOUR
Gull Lake

What more can a lake offer?

either yesterday?
with its supply of fish and game - nearby sugar bush forests - location on the Crow Wing cut-off route with access north and south - and easy availability to wild rice lakes and streams -

or today?
    With its clear water - majestic beauty - good walleye fishing - expansive opportunity for boat travel - nearness to "full service" communities - and as the location for dozens of resorts with complete recreation opportunities!
    Surely, it is one of Minnesota's finest lakes.
    As with the tales of our other lakes, we begin with the unknown. There had to be a first person to come upon Gull Lake - but we really don't know whether he - or she - came upon this inspirational setting two thousand years ago or ten thousand years ago. When the first white man arrived he probably found the Ojibway living here. We know that before the Ojibway, the Dakotas called Gull Lake home for a century or more. But who was here before the Dakotas? Did the Mandans or Gros Ventres stop here on their way west? Many think they did. We are quite certain that the lake was inhabited, off and on, for several thousands of years. We believe the Indians of the Blackduck Culture arrived sometime around 1000 A.D. But before that??? Only burial mounds and the remains of what were probably earthen dwellings give mute testimony to the Sioux and pre-Sioux era. Arrow and spear heads are still occasionally found. Not only was game killed, but human blood was probably also shed here as tribe after tribe fought to conquer or defend this "Shangri-La."
    We don't know the names of the Sioux chiefs who ruled here (up until 1739 when the Ojibway drove the Dakotas from the lake region), but it is likely that Chief Crow and the "Little Crows" who followed at least visited Gull Lake. Some of the Indian expeditionary forces we have told about in our talks of Leech Lake, Mille Lacs Lake, and the Crow Wing River crossed this body of water, including the Ojibways who stole from the dying trader at Pillager Creek, and the Rum River band of Sioux on their way north in 1768 to sack the Ojibway capital village at Sandy Lake. In later years, the Leech Lake and Sandy Lake Ojibways often used Gull Lake as a point of rendezvous on their way to and from their winter hunting grounds on the Long Prairie and Crow Wing Rivers.
    From 1739 to 1770, Gull Lake was a part of the "no man's land" populated by Sioux and Ojibway war parties. The only camp fires on its shores during those years were of men on the warpath.
    After their great victory over the Dakotas in 1766, the Ojibway began to settle northern Minnesota and there were probably villages estabished on Gull Lake by 1770.
    The first Ojibway chief to make his mark at Gull Lake was the legendary Ba-be-sig-undi-bay or "Curly Head." He was the principal chief of the Gull Lake and Crow Wing bands and provided the leadership which made it possible to hold this area against the repeated attacks by the Sioux. Curly Head was a contemporary and ally of Flat Mouth - the great Leech Lake chieftain. The two joined forces on at least one occasion to

wage war on the Dakotas[1] when a raiding party was organized to avenge the deaths of Flat Mouth's nephew and two of Curly Head's allies - Waub-o-jeeg II and She-shebe.[2]

Waub-o-jeeg III was a sub chief of the next generation whose village was located at the base of Squaw Point where he guarded the strategic source of the Gull River. The north end of the lake was under Ma-cou-da "Bear's Heart." There were as many as five separate villages on Gull Lake, each with its own chief.

In Curly Head's last years he was served by two protege's - brothers - whom he named as his "pipe bearers:" the older of the brothers (by two years) was Song-a-cumig, or "Firm Ground," and the other was to become the famous Pugona-geshig or Hole-in-the-Day I.

The brothers had come to Minnesota with the Cass Expedition in 1820, for which they were awarded medals by this famous governor of the Michigan Territory. Although younger than Firm Ground, Hole-in-the-Day was the more dynamic and out-going. Before the 1820's were over, he had been named a sub-chief at Sandy Lake and, shortly after the death of Curly Head (caused by a disease contracted at the negotiations of the 1825 Prairie du Chien Treaty) he moved with his young family to Gull Lake and soon took over as the principal chief of the Indians of that lake and the Crow Wing River. He is believed to have had his headquarters on the thoroughfare between Gull and Round Lakes. Hole-in-the-Day gathered his rice in the small lake nearby which now bears his name and collected sap from the maple trees in the wooded area between Round Lake and Long Lake[3] - now Ojibway Park.

Historian Carl Zapffe in his book, "The Man Who Lived in Three Centuries," gives an enlightening account of collaboration between the hero of his work, John Smith, and Chief Hole-in-the-Day. It seems Hole-in-the-Day's medicine man had a vision of a Sioux village which could be easily conquered and said that he could lead his chief to its location. Hole-in-the-Day asked John Smith if he cared to join him. Zapffe gives this account of Smith's response and the expedition that followed:

"Not forgetting my early pledge to spill the blood of those who had murdered my sister and brother," later recorded Smith, "I consented gladly; and, summoning all the warriors of my then great tribe, we started out upon the warpath." The combined assault was headed by Hole-in-the-Day, though guided by the Medicine Man. Three days passed in transit; and on the morning of the fourth the stage of the stealthy approach began.

Sure enough! Exactly in the position predicted by the Medicine Man, there stood a Dakota village, lying peaceably in a small valley. From one of the lodges issued a thin and lazy column of smoke. Otherwise there was no noise, neither any signs of life.

Creeping with exceeding precaution, the warriors came within gunshot, and the Chief gave the fatal signal. A simultaneous volley thundered down the little valley, lead balls pouring with well-considered spacing into every one of the tepees. The only answer was the dismal howl of a dog.

Because Smith's sole purpose in agreeing to accompany Hole-in-the-Day was to discover an opportunity for revenging the deaths in his family, he now boldly stepped forward to take the initiative in bringing this battle to its hoped-for climax.

[1]See page 30.

[2]Waub-o-jeeg, She-shebe and their families were killed and scalped while ice fishing at Mille Lacs. She-shebe is remembered for his heroic actions at Battle Point on Cross Lake, where a camp of Ojibway returning to Sandy Lake and Mille Lacs from their winter's hunt were ambushed and nearly annihilated (about 1800). The Sioux war party consisted of nearly 400 braves while the Ojibway had only half that number including the women and children.

[3]Nicollet called it "Lake Sibley", in honor of the man who was to become Minnesota's first state Governor two decades later.

Furthermore, deep inside he felt extremely confident "that no enemy bullet could kill me, as I hold a charmed life."

Not waiting to reload his gun, and grabbing nothing but his battleaxe, Smith raced to the nearest lodge — the one having a slight issue of smoke. He bounded right through the doorway, and with such fierce energy as calculated to take any opponent by surprise. But he found nothing except the dog. The exciting wisps of smoke were issuing from a few lazy embers, apparently remaining from a fire that had been abandoned hours before. Plunging his tomahawk into the body of the unfortunate dog, Smith dashed back outside and ordered his warriors to search the village. All dwellings proved to be empty.

Hole-in-the-Day was so intensely angered over this useless enterprise that he immediately killed "Big Medicine Man."

After spending a few years at Gull Lake, Hole-in-the-Day moved south to the mouth of the Crow Wing and, later, to the mouth of the Little Elk River, just north of the site of present-day Little Falls. Here he protected the southern frontier of the Ojibways. At times the pressures from the Sioux were too much and he would be forced to retreat to Whitefish or Rabbit Lake. So far as we know, he never did return to Gull Lake to live.

In 1838, Hole-in-the-Day played a major role in a series of bloody confrontations between the Dakotas and the Ojibway. In April of that year, he and a party of nine braves stumbled onto a camp of Sioux on the Chippewa River (a tributary of the Minnesota); they were mostly women and children temporarily separated from a hunting party. Professing peace, they were warmly welcomed and dined on dog meat - one of the Indians' choice delicacies. That night, on signal, Hole-in-the-Day and his men fell on the Sioux and killed all but three.

On August 2, Sioux relatives of the massacre victims had an opportunity for revenge. They surprised Hole-in-the-Day and five companions near Fort Snelling; one of the Indians with whom Hole-in-the-Day had exchanged clothing - or ornaments - was killed and another wounded (both were Ottawas). When one of the Sioux ran in to collect what he believed to be the scalp of Hole-in-the-Day, White Fisher, who was in the Ojibway party, shot him. The famous Indian Agent, Taliaferro, came on the scene at that point, and the Sioux fled. The Chippewa were taken to the fort and the Ottawa Indian was buried there. Hole-in-the-Day was escorted across the river and had to find his way home on his own.

When they heard of the incident, the chiefs of the neighboring Sioux villages came to the fort, as well as the leadership of the Red Wing band of Lake Pepin - to which the young Sioux belonged who had killed the Ottawa.

At the insistence of the commander of the fort, Major Plympton, two young braves were turned over to him and placed in custody, but the chiefs pleaded for their lives. After being satisfied that the Sioux leadership would properly punish their young warriors, Major Plympton released them to their custody. The punishment administered by the ranking Sioux braves to the culprits was traditional: their blankets, leggings and breech cloths were cut into small pieces; their hair was cut short (signifying great humiliation); and they were heavily flogged. One Ojibway was dead; one Sioux was dead; the score was even, and it seemed peace would be continued.

However, the following year, 1839, Hole-in-the-Day with five hundred of his own people, another hundred from the Crow Wing area, one hundred fifty from Leech Lake, and another contingent from Mille Lacs Lake all arrived at the St. Peter's Agency (by the fort) under the mistaken notion that they could collect certain annuities due them. Twelve hundred Sioux arrived at the agency for the same purpose (but under a different treaty). The Ojibway were told they would have to go to La Pointe to collect what they had coming, but they were given some food. Surprisingly enough, the historic enemies got along well and even danced and played games together. After a month, the food ran out and the Ojibway began their return journeys to the north. Two of Hole-in-the-Day's men who were related to the warrior shot the previous year stopped at the fort to weep over the grave of their slain kinsman. Inspired to seek revenge, they approached the Lake Calhoun camp of the Dakotas at night- some think with the knowledge and encouragement of Hole-in-the-Day. At daybreak they killed a departing hunter named Nika. The slain Sioux turned out to be a highly respected warrior, brother-in-law of the chief, and nephew of the famous medicine man, Red Bird.

Revenge came quickly. One contingent of about one hundred warriors - under Little Crow (a predecessor of the Little Crow who led the Sioux uprising in 1862) - surprised a large band of Ojibway near the present site of Stillwater. They were finally driven off but not before killing twenty-one and wounding twenty-nine Ojibway. The second contingent, under Red Bird, pursued the Mille Lacs Lake band. Before leaving the pipe of war was passed down the rows of Sioux warriors and Red Bird followed, laying hands on the heads of each and swearing them to strike without pity, taking no captives. After locating the Mille Lacs Indians, they waited until most braves had gone on ahead to hunt. The old men, women, and children left behind were at first easy prey, but the hunters returned quickly and a bitter struggle ensued. The Sioux took seventy scalps but lost seventeen braves of their own, including Red Bird and his son. The Ojibway scalps were hung from their lodge poles at Lake Calhoun and the celebrating went on for a month.

Taliaferro was keenly disappointed and left the agency soon thereafter. He had taken a special interest and pride in the Lake Calhoun settlement where he had been quite successful in encouraging agricultural practices. He had given the settlement the name "Eatonville." And so the bloody conflict between the two great tribes continued for another generation.[1]

Chief Hole-in-the-Day died in 1847 at an age of about forty-six years. He was returning from Pigs Eye (St. Paul) where he had consumed so much firewater he was being carried home prostrate on the floor of a wagon. As the entourage was crossing the Platte River he fell from the wagon and was critically injured. His warriors carried him to a nearby home; here he regained consciousness long enough to pass on the mantle of authority and a few words of wisdom to his son - Kwi-wi-sens (or "Boy"). When he died, he was buried according to his instructions on Baldur Bluff - overlooking the Mississippi. Here, in death, he continued his vigil for the canoes of the Sioux.

Carl Zapffe tells us in his book, "The Man Who Lived in Three Centuries," that in 1971, when the Little Falls-Brainerd-Staples area was deluged by the greatest cloudburst of recorded time - washing out sections of Highway #10 and the Burlington Northern Railroad tracks and isolating northern Minnesota for more than a day - many recalled the "legend of Hole-In-the-Day's promise."

Shortly before his fateful trip to St. Paul, he is said to have prophesied his death and promised that if he were buried on his beloved high bluff, his spirit would brood over the area and protect it from storms. According to meteorlogical record, the area near his burial place was free from any tornadoes or devastating storms until the 1971

[1]Warren, William, History of the Ojibway, Minnesota Historical Collection, Vol. 5.

deluge. Interestingly enough, it was in that year that new highway construction came within fifty yards of the granite stone that marks his grave. Was the spirit of Hole-in-the-Day warning that his resting place must not be disturbed? ? ?

Hole-in-the-Day's older brother, Song-a-cumig (Firm Ground) chose a less dramatic role but was a chief in his own right. We know that he and his brother worked as a team and that he won fame as a warrior. The brothers deserve credit for repulsing every Sioux attempt to re-enter the lower lake region. When he died (before his fiftieth birthday) he was eligible to wear thirty-eight feathers in his headdress, each one symbolizing the death of a Dakota Indian.

With the passing of his father, Kwi-wi-sens ("Boy") became the principal chief of the Gull Lake and Crow Wing Ojibway. He took his father's name as his own and we remember him as Chief Hole-in-the-Day II (or "the younger") - the last of the major Ojibway chiefs. That is not to say that great Ojibway leadership has not followed, but after Hole-in-the-Day the power base was gone. Indian lands had been signed away in treaty after treaty and the rout of the Sioux in 1863 left white man clearly in control of Minnesota and the destiny of the American Indian.

Hole-in-the-Day had headquarters at both the mouth of the Crow Wing and at his boyhood home on Gull Lake. It is believed by some that the log cabin located at Highway 371 and the Mission Road was his (later, Chief Wadena's). He also built a cabin several hundred yards east of his father's earlier home in Ojibway Park - between Round and Long Lakes.

Old Hole-in-the-Day had raised "Boy" to be tough, hard, and aggressive. When a lad not yet in his teens (1838), his father "arranged" for him to stab and scalp a Sioux girl of about the same age.

By 1855, Hole-in-the-Day II was recognized by the Whites as the principal chief of the Gull Lake-Crow Wing Ojibway - and was so designated in the treaty signed that year establishing the Gull Lake reservation. This action was not well received by all Ojibway. Some of the Gull Lake leadership was especially unhappy and Kwi-wi-sens-ish or "Bad Boy," was sufficiently disgruntled to leave Gull a couple of years later and take up residence at Mille Lacs Lake.

Hole-in-the-Day got the attention of Territorial Governor Ramsey and most Minnesotans in 1850 when he and a small party (perhaps only one or two others) attack six Sioux (taking one scalp) just across the river from St. Paul (after hiding in the gorge of Fountain Cave). The attack was probably in reprisal for the Sioux annihilation of a party of fifteen Ojibway a little more than a month earlier on the Apple River in Wisconsin. Governor Ramsey summoned the chiefs of both the Sioux and the Ojibway to a peace council at Fort Snelling. On June 9th, Hole-in-the-Day arrived with about 100 braves; late the following morning about 300 Sioux arrived on horseback; they dismounted in a display of pagentry and saluted the Ojibway who had lined up to welcome them. Governor Ramsey presided personally at the council. William Warren, the Ojibway historian whom we have quoted so liberally, read the charges against the Sioux, and Bad Hail, read the counter-charges against the Ojibway. All sides finally agreed to abide by the provisions of the treaty of 1843 and the council concluded with a feast.

Earlier in the proceedings the Sioux Chiefs had left the council in protest of the presence of some white women who were on hand as members of the Governor's

[1]The "ish" in Bad Boy's Indian name means "bad" and it may be that it was Ojibway that we have acquired this expression indicating something undesireable.

Chief Hole-in-the-Day, the Younger. He cut a wide swath across the pages of 19th century Ojibway history.

MINNESOTA IN 1852

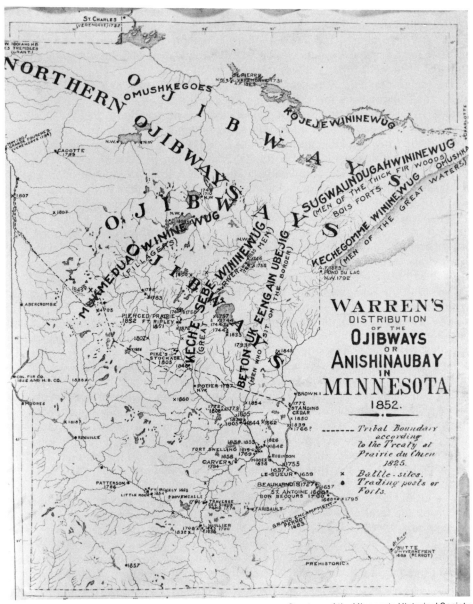

party. Hole-in-the-Day scored a coup by offering the women seats among his people. However, the women thought it best to leave, and when the Sioux returned they were sharply taken to task by Governor Ramsey. But the council concluded peacefully and to the satisfaction of the Governor, but mistrust on both sides was still evident as hostages were required to insure safe journeys home.

When our Civil War broke out, the American Indian was anxious, puzzled, and tempted. He had seen white man's governments topple before. The British had replaced the French and the American "Long Knives" had replaced the British and in 1812 the British had threatened to reclaim their lost ground. Was the Great White Father in Washington on the way out? White civilization had not given the Indian much cause to rejoice; if there would ever be an opportunity to reclaim his old lands and rid the area of the white man - it was then.

The Minnesota Sioux were probably less fearful of White man as a result of the Civil War. The Ojibway were not so sure, but Hole-in-the-Day II was apparently ready to take a chance. Historians do not agree whether or not there was collaboration between these age-old rival tribes, but there is some circumstantial evidence that Chiefs Little Crow and Hole-in-the-Day conspired. At any rate, on the very same day, August 18, 1862, the Sioux and the Ojibway swung into action more than one hundred miles apart. The simultaneous attacks, according to historian Carl Zapffe, were supposedly timed for the middle day of the three-day dark of the moon period which occurs monthly - when there is no moon at all, all night long.

There was at least one important difference in the two attacks - Little Crow had the support of the vast majority of his people; Hole-in-the-Day controlled only the Gull Lake-Crow Wing area. However, he had been in negotiation with the Ojibway at Leech Lake, Battle Lake and elsewhere and thought he could count on their support. If he had been correct in his assumption, northern Minnesota would have been subjected to the same bloodbath as the Minnesota River Valley. As it was, southern Minnesota became the setting for the most devastating massacre in the nation's history. These atrocities, plus the annihilation of Custer and his men at Little Big Horn and the culmination of white man's reprisals at Wounded Knee, taken together, are the most deplorable chapter in the history of White - Indian relations.

As with all wars, there were direct causes or incidents which triggered the fighting and then the more significant indirect causes. Let us examine the latter, first. The Sioux had many reasons for dissatisfaction and concern: (1) there was an obvious westward movement of Whites with a ravenous hunger for land; (2) Indian policies of the United States Government were disheartening - treaty payments were late[1] and meager. Indian Agents were political appointees, often ill prepared for their jobs, and the Indians were literally compressed into reservations; and (3) the very nature of the Sioux people, at least at that time, was warlike and aggressive and they were not accustomed to being pushed around without fighting back.

The incident that triggered this war was the killing of five whites by four Wahpeton braves on the farm of Howard Baker near Acton. Understanding the significance of the murders, the Sioux debated long into the night what course of action to take. Tradition holds that Little Crow opposed further violence against the Whites, comparing the White soldiers who would come for revenge to "clouds of locusts." If this is true, then the theory of collaboration with Chief Hole-in-the-Day is somewhat

[1]Many believe that the uprising could have been averted if the treaty payments had been on time or even arrived the day before the revolt.

Chief Little Crow in 1858—general of the great Sioux uprising in 1862.

Courtesy of the Minnesota Historical Society

discredited. At any rate, it has been said that Little Crow yielded to his hot-blooded braves in fear that they would turn elsewhere for leadership. They had already turned not long before to another called "Traveling Hail" for "chief speaker." And so the die was cast and the balance of the night was spent in preparation for attack. The next day, August 18, 1862, Little Crow lead about two hundred warriors against the Redwood Indian Agency. Victory came easily.

There is every evidence that the Whites of Minnesota were completely surprised by the uprising. Frontier newspapers of the day gave no indication of immediate concern, even though it was common knowledge that the treaty payments due the Dakotas were long overdue.

Sioux victories came quickly following the success at the Lower Agency; (1) of forty-six soldiers who followed Captain John Marsh out of Fort Ridgely on their way to Redwood, more than half, including the captain, perished; (2) more than fifty members of German farm families in Brown and Nicollet Counties were also killed on the first day; (3) New Ulm was attacked twice - but survived;[1] (4) more than eight hundred Sioux lay siege to Fort Ridgely - but the fort held; and (5) at the ambush at Birch Coulee, more than eighty soldiers were killed. Estimates ran as high as five hundred[2] Whites killed and a thousand wounded; the number of Indian casualities remains unknown. But in a matter of weeks it was all over.

Sibley amassed an army of more than 1600 men; many more were in reserve. Sheer numbers made it just a matter of time until the Sioux would have to accept the futility of their uprising. The Battle of Wood Lake was fought on September 23. Although a massive action, only seven soldiers were killed or died later as a result. There was a futile Sioux attack on Fort Abercrombie a few days later, followed by isolated skirmishes, but the war was over. Little Crow[3] and his surviving warriors fled to the Dakotas and Canada. The Battle of the Little Big Horn and the tragedy of Wounded Knee were yet to come, along with dozens of smaller skirmishes, but for Minnesotans there would be only one more armed clash between Whites and Indians - and that would be at Leech Lake thirty-six years later.

As an aftermath to the war, more than 300 Sioux prisoners are condemned to death. Because of the huge number, Sibley decided to share the burden of decision by referring the final judgement to General Pope. The general, in turn, passed it on to that desk "where the buck always stops" - to President Lincoln, himself. Even though already heavily burdened by the great Civil War, President Lincoln ordered a review of each case, individually, and expressed his desire that no man should die merely because he participated in the war. Only those who had murdered civilians or were guilty of rape (just two cases) were to pay with their lives. Finally, on Lincoln's written orders, thirty-eight Sioux warriors were hanged, simultaneously, in Mankato on December 26, 1862.

[1]More than ninety buildings were burned—some in defense of the city.

[2]Four hundred eighty-six is the accepted estimate by today's historians.

[3]Following the uprising a $500 price was placed on Little Crow's head and the state paid bounties for Sioux scalps. Little Crow returned to Minnesota with a few braves and was killed by a hunting party near Hutchinson. The reward was collected by Nathan Lawson. His body was identified by his deformed hands and wrists, the result of a quarrel with his brothers over who would become chief following the death of his father. He became the third "Little Crow" of his tribe. When the bullet had passed through his wrists, he had gone to Fort Snelling for help. The surgeon suggested amputation. Little Crow decided to gamble, and with the help of his own medicine men and "mother nature" he was able to use his hands. He was killed on July 3, 1863. The next day his body was dragged through the streets of Hutchinson as part of the July 4th celebration and finally cast on the city dump. Later he was buried in St. Paul. More than 100 years later he was re-buried by the Big Sioux River near Flandreau, So. Dakota.

As Little Crow was leading the Dakotas against the Redwood Agency, Hole-in-the-Day was at the very same time directing the obliteration of the St. Columba Mission by several hundred Ojibway warriors who had been gathered from as far as Sandy Lake to the east and Ottertail on the west. Why did the wiley Chieftain choose the little church on the shores of Gull Lake as the subject of his first attack when he could have chosen strategic Fort Ripley or the white settlement of Crow Wing? First of all, the mission not only symbolized white man but it also represented his foreign religion. Secondly, Hole-in-the-Day may have been waiting for the expected reinforcements from Leech Lake. If, in truth, there was collaboration between the Sioux and the Ojibway, he may have felt compelled to do something dramatic on the agreed day but did not want to risk defeat at another location while he was waiting for substantial reinforcements.

The burning of the mission was a cheap victory. The white clergy had been frightened away from the work at Gull Lake five years earlier in 1857 and had left it in the care of a native deacon, John Johnson or Emmegahbowh. The faithful Ottawa Indian and his family had taken flight by canoe to Crow Wing and then Fort Ripley the night before the attack. Although not a long journey, two of Emmegahbowh's younger children are said to have died from the rigors of the trip.

Flush with the satisfaction of the successful completion of his act of defiance, Hole-in-the-Day was reported to have been anxious for the arrival of the Leech Lake Pillagers so he could proceed with his planned attack against the village of Crow Wing, Fort Ripley, St. Cloud and - perhaps - on to join forces with the Sioux. But the leadership of the Leech Lake bands were having second thoughts. The younger warriors, eager for battle, had quickly taken the few whites in the area into captivity and proposed a public execution. However, two respected chiefs, Buffalo and Big Dog[1], were not so sure Hole-in-the-Day would be the eventual victor. Wisely they persuaded their braves to bring the captives to Gull Lake, reasoning that if Hole-in-the-Day had changed his mind or had not been successful, the Leech Lake Indians would be left alone to feel the wrath of the Whites. After a two day journey, they arrived at the appointed rendezvous between Round Lake and Gull Lake. Here they found Hole-in-the-Day less sure of his plan and the captives were eventually released.

Several things had happened. When Deacon Emmegahbowh and his family reached Crow Wing and Fort Ripley, panic was the natural reaction. Major Walker, Indian Agent near the village, took off alone for St. Paul; he was later found dead along the trail. It is believed that he committed suicide. Other Whites and mixed bloods pleaded with the Indians of the area not to join in the uprising. Clement Beaulieu, the trading post operator-who was highly respected by Hole-in-the-Day-and George Sweet of the then tiny village of St. Cloud made a direct appeal to the chief. Father Pierz courageously entered the armed camp and confronted the leadership head-on. Another hero-and perhaps the most effective in dissuading the Ojibway from continuing on the warpath-was Chief Bad Boy of Mille Lacs Lake. As we said, he had left Gull Lake a few years before in a spirit of deep resentment because Hole-in-the-Day had been recognized by the white government as head chief of the area. Ironically, it was now the chief who had been passed over by the Whites who helped save the lives of hundreds of white settlers. Bad Boy and the other Mille Lacs chiefs

[1]Flat Mouth I had died, and his son had not yet been accepted as a principal chief.

Oua-wi-sain-shish (Bad Boy). He may have been "Bad Boy" to Hole-in-the-Day but he was a hero to the whites of central Minnesota.

marched on Fort Ripley - but not to wage war as was first thought by the panic striken settlers - but, rather to offer their support and, if necessary, even to join in battle against Hole-in-the-Day. Further, he sent a messenger directly to the Gull Lake chieftain advising him of his decision. Hole-in-the-Day may have been a lot of things, but he was not stupid. Reluctantly, but wisely, he permitted the abortion of the campaign.

If Hole-in-the-Day had been successful in organizing all of the Ojibway and had proceeded with his original plans and perhaps even joined forces with the Sioux, it would have only postponed the inevitable white victory for a little while, but thousands, instead of hundreds, of Whites and Indians would have perished.

Earlier - in the 1950's - Hole-in-the-Day had been granted an acreage of land and a sizable home had been constructed for him in return for certain considerations in the treaty negotiations. Here he lived out his years with his wives - one of them white - until his death along a trail near his home.

ST. COLUMBA MISSION

Explorers came to Minnesota for fame and adventure. Traders were interested in profit. But the missionaries were interested in bringing the Good News of the Gospel to the American Indians. The handful of God's servants who unselfishly and courageously worked among the Minnesota Indians and white settlers in the 17th, 18th, and 19th centuries have never received the full credit they deserved for the role they played in the development of our state and nation. Their letters and diaries reveal the agonies and anxieties they suffered. They realized they might very well be called on to even give their lives; and Father Alneau[1] did.

Among these spiritual giants was the Reverend James Lloyd Breck, Episcopal clergyman, who established the St. Columba Mission on the southern shores of Gull Lake in 1852. His work was relatively encouraging, but he was attracted to the much larger population of Ojibway on Leech Lake and moved there in November of 1856. But here he met frustration and bitter disappointment. He described the Pillagers as "so drunk and disorderly" that his efforts were in vain. He gave up his work only eight months after his arrival and actually left in fear of his life.

When Breck transferred his efforts to Leech Lake, other missionaries apparently carried on the work for a few months, but Breck's Ottawa assistant, John Johnson (Emmegahbowh), ended up in charge. He was both dedicated and capable, and fulfilled his duties until the night before the burning of the mission by Hole-in-the-Day's army. He was later ordained a priest and continued his work among the Ojibway, particularly at White Earth. In his later years, he also served his people as a government agent.

LOGGING DAYS

As in most parts of Minnesota, a conglomorate of lumbermen opened the country and harvested the timber. Pillsbury, Chase, Leavitt, and Horn, all of Minneapolis, were the principal owners of the Gull Lake forests.

In 1889, a short-lived narrow gauge railroad was constructed north and west of the lake under the corporate name of "Gull Lake and Northern Railway Co.," with Charles Pillsbury as President. The logs it carried were dumped into Lake Margaret

[1]See page 11.

and herded in rafts - by steamboats[1] - across Gull Lake and then down-river to the waiting saw mills of the Gull River Lumber Company. The mills were located near the place where the Northern Pacific Railroad (now Burlington Northern) crosses Gull River on the route between Brainerd and Staples. Here, in 1880, the village of Gull River became the first incorporated community in Cass County. Brainerd (called "New Town" by the Indians) had been platted in 1871. At their peak, the Gull River Mills employed 150 men and the community included more than twenty houses, an office building, a boarding house, and a general store. In 1893, the mill was moved to Rice Lake in Northeast Brainerd and today, not a trace remains of the once bustling frontier town.

Meanwhile, another and more permanent railroad - this one of standard gauge - was constructed across the Mississippi from Northeast Brainerd and from there north to Lake Hubert Station. From here it continued north through Smiley (now Nisswa), Sibley (now Pequot Lakes), Jenkins, Pine River, Mildred, Backus, the ghost towns of Lothrop and Cyphers, and finally reached Walker in 1896. During the next two years (1897-99) it pushed north to Bemidji and eventually to International Falls. Known first as the Brainerd and Northern Minnesota Railway, it was purchased by the Minnesota and International Railroad. The Northern Pacific eventually came to operate the railroad and finally took over ownership in 1942. Today it is a part of the Burlington Northern system. With the construction of this railroad, it was possible to carry much of the eastern Gull Lake area timber south by rail rather than by water. The tracks now lead north out of West Brainerd and even the historic trestle in Northeast Brainerd which carried the tracks across the Mississippi and in later years served as a bridge for

[1]Stewart Mills, a leading Brainerd businessman who today (1977) is President of the large Fleet Store chain, piloted one of these steamboats early in the century, reminding us that the great logging days of our state were really not so long ago after all. He also operated a ferry service between the railroad and the west end of the lake.

En-Me-Ga-Bow (The Rev. John Johnson), An Ottowa Indian, custodian of St. Columba Mission and Episcopal clergyman.

Courtesy of the Minnesota Historical Society

St. Columba Indian Mission of Gull Lake, sketched in 1852. It was Hole-in-the-Day's first target.

THE GULL RIVER LUMBER CO.'S PLANT AT GULL RIVER, MINN.—[From a sketch by Krause.

Gull River Lumber Company, Gull River, 1888, once located near the bridge where the Burlington Northern Railroad now crosses the river enroute from Brainerd to Staples.

present Highway 25 - is gone. A concrete bridge now spans the river at that location.

By 1911, Gull Lake had seen the last of the huge rafts of logs and a dam was constructed near the source of Gull River - forever sealing off the great log waterway.

A NEW ERA ON THE LAKE - RECREATION

The first indication of interest in Gull Lake for recreational purposes came with the construction of a "club house" by several Brainerd citizens on the thoroughfare between Gull and Round Lakes in 1895.

In 1913, only two years after the last logs were laboriously tugged across the lake, a small band of visionary men purchased the area where the St. Columba Mission once stood and plotted it into lots for summer homes. They were J.M. Elder, W.A. Barrows (for whom the now extinct mining village south of Brainerd was named), Carl Zapffe (father of the Carl Zapffe who has authored "The Man Who Lived in Three Centuries" and author, himself, of a history of Brainerd) and D.L. Fairchild (a mining engineer from Duluth). Actually, all members of the group had a common interest in mining. They called the development "St. Colombo."

Up until 1915, when these first summer homes were completed, there were no more than fifty shacks, cabins, and farms on the shores of Gull Lake. However, following the development of the St. Colombo site, other Brainerd business and professional men soon began to look to Gull and other lakes as locations for summer homes and recreation other than hunting and fishing. And so with this small beginning, the now famous Gull Lake recreation area was on its way. In summer, more than 10,000 people now live around the lake and many (the more fortunate) have year-around homes. It has become, perhaps, the second most[1] prestigious lake address in Minnesota. For example, at least three Minnesota Governors have had homes on the lake - Floyd Olson, Luther Youngdahl, and C. Elmer Anderson.

Resorts began to spring up around the lake in the 1920's and thirties. Names like Maddens, Roberts, Ruttgers, Craguns, Framptons, Bar Harbor,[2] and Grand View became nationally known.

M.B. Baker was founder of the first major resort on Gull Lake; he called it "Grand View Lodge." Located on the north end of the lake and opened about 1918, it continues to serve thousands each year. Later it was sold to F.B. Cote who expanded the facility; Cote also operated Camp Hubert for Girls and Camp Lincoln for Boys on nearby Lake Hubert.

In 1926, Walter Frampton, a Brainerd railroad machinist, opened Island View Lodge on the south end of Gull Lake; ever since, this part of Gull Lake has been the focal pont for resort activity.

It took two men from Kansas City to really recognize the recreational potential of this magnificent lake - John W. Harrison and Chester T. Start. Together they constructed the first Pine Beach Golf Course. It was no small undertaking to carve greens and fairways out of a wilderness of pine and birch. Every available farmer who owned a team of horses was hired to help - 100 teams in all! Harrison and Start were the first incorporators of Pine Beach Golf, Inc. and Pine Beach, Inc. More money was needed and Arthur Roberts, a nephew of Kahler - the Rochester Hotel Magnate - purchased about twenty-five percent of the stock. A number of Brainerd business and professional men also invested. It was then called the Brainerd Pine Beach Hotel Company.

[1]Only Lake Minnetonka may be more prestigious.

[2]The original Bar Harbor was a widely known ballroom and slot machine "super market." The building burned to the ground and a supper club with the same name is now in operation across the road. (East end of the lake)

In 1929, the large resort hotel opened on Pine Beach (first called "Brainerd Pine Beach Hotel," then "Robert's Pine Beach Hotel," and now "Madden's Inn"). The timing couldn't have been worse; both men lost a great deal of money during the great depression - Start even suffered a nervous breakdown.

In spite of the bad times, Max Ruttger purchased property from Pine Beach, Inc., in 1930 and opened his resort in 1931. The "Madden" name along with the "Ruttger" - among the best known names today in Midwest resort circles - was first associated with Gull Lake in this same year. Jack Madden opened a soda fountain and a cigar counter on Ruttger's porch in 1931. He owned his own business and paid Ruttger a percentage "of the take" as rent.

The next year, 1932, Jack Madden operated the Pine Beach Golf Course for Start and Harrison and their incorporators; he moved his soda fountain and cigar counter there as well. In 1933, Madden purchased the golf course and his brother, Jim, went to work for him at that time. Jim Madden entered the partnership in 1936; the partnership now includes John Arnold as well. Maddens were originally from Stillwater; Arnold from Brainerd.

Maddens built on Mission Point - so called because missionaries came here from St. Columba to try to convert the Indians who resided at the south end of the Lake. (but without much success) And thus began a great American success story - which today includes a resort complex serving more than 500 vacationers daily.

History buffs will enjoy visiting Madden's Lumbertown - part of the Pine Beach development-which represents a typical Minnesota lumbertown of the 1870's. The concept occurred to the Maddens while visiting Knott's Berry Farm in California. About all that are missing are the saloons and brothel houses. It is difficult to comprehend the volume of liquor traffic in those days; Stillwater, for example, had 110 saloons when it was a logging boomtown!

Other fine resorts that developed on the south end of the lake before World War I include Craguns and Coronobles.

Ruttgers is now called Pine Portage.

The virgin pine forests have been gone long enough to have been replaced by a beautiful blend of mature, second-growth pines and hardwoods. The thirty-eight miles of picturesque shoreline combined with 9,400 acres of clear water, truly make Gull Lake one of America's finest.

Roberts original Pine Beach Hotel.   Courtesy of the Minnesota Historical Society

When you want to live forever! A smiling Mike Mergens poses with his trophy walleye. There are even bigger lunkers lurking in the depths of Gull Lake.

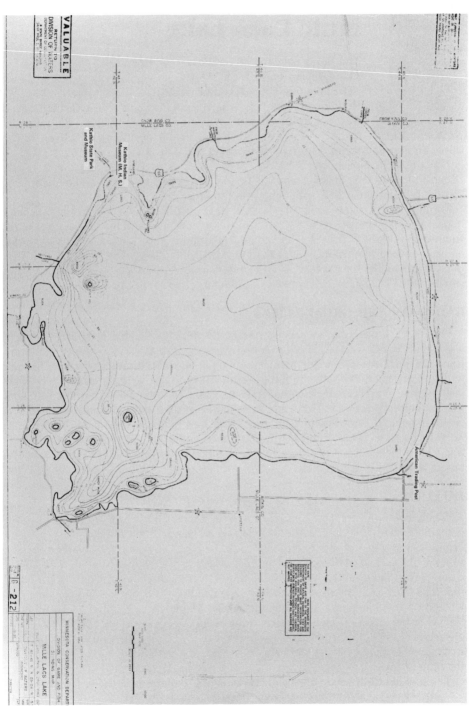

Courtesy of the Minnesota Department of Natural Resources

CHAPTER FIVE
Mille Lacs Lake

The Sioux called it "M'de'Wakan" or Spirit Lake.
The Ojibway knew it as "Missi-sag-i-egan," which is translated,
"The lake that spreads out all over."
Both loved it enough to sacrifice scores and scores of their bravest
warriors to possess it. William Warren, Ojibway himself, concluded, "There is not a spot in the northwest which an Indian
would sooner choose as a home and dwelling place."[1]

The name by which we know it, "Mille Lacs" is of French origin and means
"thousand lakes." It initially referred to the entire region but eventually came to
identify this particular lake - the largest in the area.

Formed 10,000 years ago by the last glacier to invade Minnesota, the lake lies like a
huge round opal between the higher plain to the northeast and the glacial ridge to the
southwest. Although considerably larger at one time, Mille Lacs still ranks second in
acreage among Minnesota's more than ten thousand lakes.[2] The historic Rum River
provides an outlet for the lake as it meanders irregularly to the south through three
smaller lakes - Ogeche, Shakopee, and Onamia - on its way to the Mississippi.

RADISSON AND GROSEILLIERS

Mille Lacs Lake may have been one of the first identifiable locations visited by
white men in Minnesota. There is some evidence that the 17th century explorers,
Radisson and Groseilliers - the French brothers-in-law who turned to England for help
and support when frustrated by the government of their own country and who were
instrumental in the formation of the Hudson's Bay Co. - may have been the first white
men to enter Minnesota. There is also evidence in their journals that they met with
Sioux Indians in a conclave which may have been held on Knife Lake, seven miles
north of Mora in 1660. If this is true, then it could be that Radisson and Groseilliers
also visited Mille Lacs at that time and were thereby the first whites to gaze across its
broad, eighteen mile expanse.

DU LUTH

Nearly twenty years later, on July 2, 1679, David Greysolon, the sieur du Lhut,
definitely visited Mille Lacs Lake. He named it "Buade" (the family name of Count
Frontenac) and in a proper ceremony - with the Sioux as witnesses - planted the coat
of arms of the King of France "in the great village of the Nadouesioux, called Izaty's,
where never had a Frenchman been." "Izatys" was incorrectly copied from Du Luth's
report as "Kathio." And thus the ancient capital of the Sioux people and the state park
located on the village site are really incorrectly identified as "Kathio." Nevertheless,
Kathio is the oldest village name in Minnesota, and was likely the home of the
ancestors of such great Sioux chiefs as Sitting Bull and Crazy Horse. Du Luth reported
that two other Sioux villages were also located on the southwest shore of Mille Lacs at
the time of his visit.

Three of Du Luth's men explored farther West - beyond Mille Lacs. No one knows

[1]Warren, William, History of the Ojibways, Minn. Historical Collection, Vol. 5.

[2]Mille Lacs has seventy-five miles of shoreline and 131,885 acres of water surface. Lower Red with 180,968
acres is the largest lake entirely within Minnesota's borders.

how far they may have gone, but they did bring back a report that "it was only twenty days journey from where they were" to a "great lake where water is not good to drink." They may have been referring to Great Salt Lake.

FATHER HENNEPIN

One year later, in 1680, the Sioux brought Father Hennepin[1] and his two colleagues - Michael Accault[2] (or Ako) and Antoine Auguelle - to Mille Lacs Lake as their prisoners. The three men had been sent by LaSalle to explore the upper regions of the Mississippi and had arrived at Lake Pepin by way of Lakes Erie, Huron, and Michigan and after visiting a French fort at the site of present-day Chicago. At Lake Pepin they encountered a large war party of Dakotas who had traveled south from their Mille Lacs area villages under the leadership of a chief named "Aquipaguetin." The chief had recently lost a son in an encounter with the Miami Indians (who headquartered around the southern end of Lake Michigan). The three whites were quickly apprehended - apparently as some sort of retribution for the lost son. It was customary for the bereaved Indian to be quite demonstrative in his mourning for the deceased - with much weeping and wailing. In this case, the chief literally wept over the heads of his captives while trying to make up his mind whether to adopt the Frenchmen as replacements for his son and other lost warriors - or kill them! In retrospect, Father Hennepin named our Lake Pepin - "The Lake of Tears." At long last the decision was made to adopt the three white men into separate Sioux families - and then began the long journey north. When the party reached the mouth of the Minnesota River, they abandoned their canoes and proceeded on foot. The march was so difficult that the explorers could not make it on their own but were often carried on the backs of the Indians - which says something about the endurance and physiques of the Sioux! Upon reaching Mille Lacs, the men were separated and went with their adopted families. Father Hennepin wrote that he was taken to an island to live. Many have assumed that he was imprisoned[3] on "Hennepin Island" - the small, rocky outcropping which lies far out in the lake and towards the eastern shore - but it is more probable that his island was actually on Lake Onamia.

Hennepin was apparently well cared for. He was treated to steam baths and massaged with wildcat oil. He was presented with "a robe made of ten large dressed beaver skins, trimmed with porcupine quills." The chief had five wives and even offered Father Hennepin the use of one or more of them for his "personal pleasure." During his short stay he was allowed to baptize a sick child (which later died) and tried to compose a dictionary of Sioux words.

The news of their "capture" reached Du Luth while he was on his way down the St. Croix River. He promptly left his party and hurried, bravely and dramatically, to their rescue. He overtook a Sioux hunting party on the Mississippi River and found Father

[1]To historians, Hennepin is a controversial figure. He is credited with authoring several works which were published and widely read in Europe. They include "Description de la Louisiana" (1683), "Nouveau Voyage" (1696), and "Nouvelle Decouverte" (1697). Much of the material was exaggerated and even not true, but defenders of the priest maintain that others made his material more exciting and more readable and that his name was merely used - particularly in the latter two works. Nevertheless, Father Hennepin made a significant contribution in his exploration and discoveries and is deserving of recognition for making much of Europe "excited" about the new world.

[2]Accault was actually the leader of this "mini-expedition" and Auguelle was his assistant.

[3]Because the men were so well treated and given considerable freedom, there is some doubt as to whether they were really "held prisoner."

Hennepin and the other Frenchmen among them - still captives, but apparently on a more friendly basis. Father Hennepin had even been allowed to explore down river to see if supplies promised by LaSalle had been delivered to the mouth of the Wisconsin River. Enroute he discovered and named the falls of St. Anthony. Du Luth, however, insisted that the party return to Mille Lacs Lake and demanded that a council meeting be called. Indignantly, he returned the peace pipes he had received from the Dakotas earlier and lectured them severely. In September Du Luth left Mille Lacs with the three Frenchmen in tow and set out for Green Bay.

The courage of Du Luth becomes even more incredible when we realize that the fierce Mille Lacs Lake warriors may never have seen a white man prior to his visit the previous year (with the possible exception of some who may have seen Radisson and Groseilliers twenty years earlier) and that Du Luth and his companions were a mere handful of men in the midst of an army of "uncivilized" Dakota warriors reknowned for their fighting ability and merciless treatment of their adversaries. On the other hand, up until then the white man had given the Sioux no cause to hate. So - where lies the truth? Did the Sioux allow Du Luth to chastise them and then take off with their captives because of their respect for the power he claimed to represent? Or were these earlier Sioux less warlike than we came to know them to be during their struggle - first against the invading Ojibway and then in a bloody protest against the treatment they had received at the hands of the whites?

Of course, the Native Americans were doubtlessly awed by the "different" appearance of their pale-faced visitors. And some went out of their way to impress the Indians; Jean Nicolet for example arrived at Green Bay dressed in an oriental damask robe and "carrying thunder in both hands."

INDIAN BEGINNINGS

Although Du Luth gave us documentary evidence that the Sioux were well established on the shores of Mille Lacs in the latter part of the 1600's, we don't know how long they had been there. Inasmuch as Kathio is usually recognized as the capital of the Sioux nation, and inasmuch as Sioux traditions indicate a long stay on the lake, it is likely the tribe inhabited its shores for many generations before Du Luth's visits. Because the Sioux moved into southern Minnesota about 1000 A.D., but did not control the northern regions of the state until the 1600's, it is difficult to estimate the time of their arrival at Mille Lacs - which although heavily wooded, really lies in between these two areas. We do know, however, that the shores of the lake have been occupied by Indians for several thousands of years - since, perhaps, not too long after the melting of the last glacier - which scientists say was about 10,000 years ago. Evidence of inhabitants dating between 3000 BC and 1000 BC have been found in Petagu Point. Examinations at the Cooper village site have indicated settlements between 1400 A.D. and 1750 A.D. Archeological explorations have been most fruitful, all the way from the Kathio village site (where the Rum River leaves the lake) to the present townsite of Onamia. Knives, awls, punches, and other tools made from copper have been found and their age has been estimated at from three to five thousand years. Other signs of ancient villages in this general area include an abundance of pottery fragments and numerous wild rice pits.

On the east side of Lake Ogeche, archeologists have uncovered the remains of another village which was at least partly enclosed by a stockade. Outlines of the dwellings have been clearly identified - some rectangular and others round with sunken floors.

Archeologists consider their diggings in the Mille Lacs Lake area to be among the most significant in the upper Mississippi region. For example, the artifacts found here give us clues to the transition of the Sioux from a plains Indian to a woodlands Indian and visa versa. A remarkable exhibit of these artifacts is on display at the Indian Museum in the park.

There is also Kathio Indian Museum on the highway near Onamia which depicts Chippewa and Sioux life through four seasons; it is operated by the Minnesota Historical Society.

The Mille Lacs Lake Dakotas, and probably their predecessors, used permanent, earthen homes as well as the more familiar hide and bark covered teepees - which were so essential to the nomadic periods of Sioux history.

But the Sioux were destined to lose their beloved "Spirit Lake" to the Ojibway. We can be sure it was not given up without much shedding of blood; however, there are some who suggest they were lured south by traders such as Le Sueur[1] and Perrot[2] and that Ojibway pressures were not the only reason for their abandonment of the lake.

According to Ojibway tradition, the Sioux were driven from their Mille Lacs Lake strongholds as a result of one great three-day battle, perhaps about the same time as they were forced from their villages on Leech, Sandy, and Gull in the 1740's. Warren[3] tells the traditional account well as he relates an interview with an old Mille Lacs-Ojibway Chieftain, probably sometime around 1850:

"There was an old man residing at Fond du Lac of Lake Superior which place had at this time, already become an important village of the Ojibways. This old man was looked upon by his people with much respect and consideration: though not a chief, he was a great hunter, and his lodge ever abounded in plenty. He belonged to the Marten Totem family. He was blessed with four sons, all of whom were full grown and likely men, "fair to look upon." They were accustomed to make frequent visits to the villages of the Dakotas, and they generally returned laden with presents, for the young women of their tribe looked on them with wishful and longing eyes.

Shortly after a quarrel about a woman had taken place, which resulted in the death of an Ojibway, the four brothers paid the Dakotas one of their usual peaceful visits; they proceeded to their great town at Mille Lac, which was but two days from their villages. During this visit, one of the brothers was treacherously murdered, and but three returned with safety to their father's wigwam.

The old man did not even complain when he heard that their former enemies had sent his son to travel on the Spirit road; and shortly after, when his three surviving sons asked his permission to go again to enter the lodges of the Dakotas, he told them

[1]Pierre Charles Le Sueur established himself as a trader along the Bruke-St. Croix waterways and worked closely with the Minnesota Sioux. He even brought a Sioux Chief to Montreal for an audience with Frontenac (the Governor General of New France.) Later he returned to France where he applied to the King for a ten year monopoly of fur trade on the Mississippi as well as mining rights. Some suspect that the mining request was thrown in to gain favorable action on his request to monopolize fur trade. Le Sueur than sailed for the mouth of the Mississippi and ascended the river with nine men (1700). It took from April to September to reach the Upper Mississippi. His fur trading was successful, but he brought back two tons of worthless blue clay (alegedly copper ore) to France. The material was mined near his headquarters (Fort L'Huillier") near the mouth of the Blue Earth River.

[2]Nicolas Perrot was named commandant of the West in 1685. He was a successful trader who established posts on the Upper Wisconsin side of the Mississippi River. He claimed possession of the upper Mississippi in the name of Louis XIV of France in 1689.

[3]Warren, William W., History of the Ojibways, Minnesota Historical Collection, Volume 5.

to go, "for probably," said he, "they have taken the life of my son through mistake." The brothers proceeded as before to Mille Lac, and on this occasion, two of them were again treacherously killed, and but one returned to the wigwam of his bereaved father. The fount of the old man's tears still did not open, though he blacked his face in mourning, and his head hung down in sorrow.

Once more his sole surviving son requested to pay the Dakotas a peace visit, that he might look on the graves of his deceased brethren. His sorrow stricken parent said to him, "go, my son, for probably they have struck your brothers through mistake." Day after day rolled over, till the time came when he had promised to return. The days, however, kept rolling on, and the young man returned not to cheer the lonely lodge of his father. A full moon passed over, and still he made not his appearance, and the old man became convinced that the Dakotas had sent him to join his murdered brethren in the land of Spirits. Now, for the first time, the bereaved father began to weep, the fount of his tears welled forth bitter drops, and he mourned bitterly for his lost children.

"An Ojibway warrior never throws away his tears," and the old man determined to have revenge. For two years he busied himself in making preparations. With the fruits of his hunts he procured ammunition and other materials for a war party. He sent his tobacco and warclub to the remotest villages of his people, detailing his wrong and inviting them to collect by a certain day at Fond du Lac, to go with him in "search for his lost children." His summons was promptly and numerously obeyed, and nearly all the men of his tribe residing on the shores of the Great Lake, collected by the appointed time at Fond du Lac. Their scalping knives had long rusted in disuse, and the warriors were eager once more to stain them with the blood of their old enemy.

Having made the customary preparations, and invoking the Great Spirit to their aid, this large war party which the old man had collected, left Fond du Lac, and followed the trail towards Mille Lac, which was then considered the strongest hold of their enemies, and where the blood which they went to revenge had been spilt. The Dakotas occupied the lake in two large villages, one being located on Cormorant point, and the other at the outlet of the lake. A few miles below this last village, they possessed another considerable village on a smaller lake, connected with Mille Lac by a portion of Rum River which runs through it. These villages consisted mostly of earthen wigwams such as are found still to be in use among the Arickarees and other tribes residing on the Upper Missouri.

The vanguard of the Ojibways fell on the Dakotas at Cormorant point early in the morning, and such was the extent of the war party, that before the rear had arrived, the battle at this point had already ended by the almost total extermination of its inhabitants; a small remnant only, retired in their canoes to the greater village located at the entry. This, the Ojibways attacked with all their forces; after a brave defence with their bows and barbed arrows, the Dakotas took refuge in their earthen lodges from the more deadly weapons of their enemy.

The only manner by which the Ojibways could harass and dislodge them from these otherwise secure retreats, was to throw small bundles or bags of powder into the aperture made in the top of each, both for the purpose of giving light within, and emitting the smoke of the wigwam fire. The bundles ignited by the fire, spread death and dismay amongst the miserable beings who crowded within. Not having as yet, like the more fortunate Ojibways, been blessed with the presence of white traders, the Dakotas were still ignorant of the nature of gunpowder, and the idea possessing their minds that their enemies were aided by spirits, they gave up the fight in despair and were easily dispatched. But a remnant retired during the darkness of night to their last remaining village on the smaller lake. Here they made their last stand, and the Ojibways following them up, the havoc among their ranks was continued during the whole course of another day.

The next morning the Ojibways wishing to renew the conflict, found the village *evacuated by the few who had survived their victorious arms. They had fled during the night down the river in their canoes, and it became a common saying that the former dwellers of Mille Lacs became, by this three days' struggle, swept away forever from their favorite village sites." They are believed to have settled at the mouth of the Rum River.*

In subsequent years, the Mille Lacs Lake Ojibway made their mark on Minnesota history. It was on the winter ice of Mille Lacs that Waub-o-jeeg and She-shebe and their families were caught off guard by the Sioux while they were fishing and were slain - thus precipitating extensive reprisals by their friends Curly Head and Flat Mouth.

It was a band of Mille Lacs Lake Ojibway in 1839 — on their way home from Fort Snelling — who were surprised by the Sioux from Lake Calhoun and lost 70 men, women and children before fighting them off.

And it was Chief Bad Boy of Mille Lacs who came to the aid of the Whites in Central Minnesota and stood up to Hole-in-the-Day in 1862 and prevented a massacre.

THE LOGGING ERA

In 1837, the United States government entered into a treaty with Minnesota Indians which included the purchase of the triangle of land formed by the St. Croix and Mississippi Rivers. Even though nearly all of Mille Lacs Lake was included in the triangle, the Ojibway did not leave the area and in 1885 the United States government established three small reservations on the southwest shore, with a combined population of several hundred Ojibway. Today, only a remnant remain on or near the lake.

The Treaty of 1837 opened the triangle of land to loggers as well as to settlers, and this really marked the beginning of the huge lumbering industry in Minnesota - an industry which was to dominate the state's economy for several decades. The forests of the Mille Lacs area were predominantly pine, but there were also hardwoods, including maple and birch. The first settlers reported that the pines were so tall and heavy that "trails were often so dark in the day time it was almost like evening." Mille Lacs Lake was along the north baseline of the inverted triangle formed by the St. Croix and Mississippi Rivers and the timber of the lake was the last to be harvested in the area included in the land-purchase. Whereas the forests in the southern end of the triangle were cut almost immediately, logging in the Mille Lacs area was not done on a large scale until the 1880's. The Rum River made the transportation of logs relatively easy for delivery to their destinations at the Minneapolis sawmills, but by the 1900's, mills began appearing along the way, including a large operation by the Foley-Bean Company at Milaca.

Verril and McGregor brought their lumbering operations to the lake in the early 1880's and located east of present-day Isle. The company built a steamboat twenty feet wide and eighty-five feet long to tow the boom-enclosed log rafts across the lake. The boat was capable of towing up to two million feet of logs in a single boom! In 1885 the firm constructed a dam on Malone Creek. Logs were stacked on ice in the winter, and when the impoundment was released in the spring there was sufficient water to float the logs out to the lake itself.

The O'Neal Brothers of Stillwater began logging operations in the Redtop area in 1888 and even constructed a railroad from Knife Lake to the shores of Mille Lacs - terminating about a half-mile from where Isle is located today. Since the railroad was isolated from any other, the locomotive had to be moved in during the winter on sections of rail laid on frozen ground.[1]

[1]Mille Lacs Lake Messenger, Golden Anniversary Issue.

Starting in 1900, the Ferguson Davis Company of Anoka logged the country northeast of Malmo.

Logging continued up to World War I, with McGrath purchasing stumpage rights to a vast area east of Wahkon in 1914, but by that time most of the logging operations had moved much farther north.

Most of these operators of the 19th and early 20th century sold their logs to the Foley-Bean Company.

EARLY WHITE SETTLERS

During the fur trading era, a French Post was established at Kathio and an American Fur Company operation was at the north end of the lake.

When the Soo Railroad arrived at the lake in 1907, it not only facilitated logging, but it also brought large numbers of settlers into the area. Actually a good number of hardy Scandinavians had arrived in the early 1880's - either on foot or with a pack horse or two. They built log homes and cleared land, but most joined logging crews as the lumbering interests moved in.

Schools and churches were among the first concerns of these immigrants, and one-room, log school houses were quickly built at Eastwood in 1884, Opstead in 1892, and Onamia in 1905. Rev. George Chase was the first protestant circuit rider to serve the lake area; he usually held services in logging camps and the farm families came from miles around. Father Dintner was one of the first Catholic Missionaries in the area; he headquartered at Onamia. One should not assume, however, that the logging operations were all that virtuous - saloons and "brothel houses" were a higher priority in the minds of many.

Prior to the coming of the railroad, there were beginnings of communities at Onamia, Cove, and Wahkon.

The first businessman among the few settlers at Onamia was a blacksmith named John De Mar.

The Wahkon site originally included two tiny communities by the names of "Pott's Town" and "Lawrence" - located side by side. The former developed around a small hotel built on the lake in 1885 by T.E. Potts. Lawrence was plotted just west of Pott's Town in 1904. With the coming of the Soo Line in 1907, a new and much larger town was laid-out which absorbed both communities and was given the name "Wahkon" (the Sioux word for "spirit" which was the name the Indians had given the lake).

Prior to the arrival of the railroad, Cove was the largest community on the lake. It was the center for logging operations and served as a "jumping off place" for settlers. The lake's first newspaper was published in Cove in 1903.

The community of Redtop is an excellent example of the scores of Minnesota boom towns that sprang up during the early logging or mining days and then died or all but disappeared. According to tradition, Redtop was named for the red-headed cook in the Haggberg Logging camp,[1] Olivia Erickson. Once larger than Isle, every business place was eventually closed.[2]

Railroad planners had enormous power over the destiny of land and population development. Railroads built up cities; the removal of rail service destroyed cities. Thus, Onamia, which boasted a single business operation (the blacksmith) in 1906, was really born with the coming of the railroad a year later, when a bank and a number of stores were immediately constructed. When the logging operations ceased, Onamia

[1]Later sold to Quackenbush Industries.
[2]Mille Lacs Lake Messenger, Golden Anniversary Issue.

Cundy's Trading Post, 1888, between Lakes Shaiopee and Onamia. The boxes in the center of the picture contain wild cranberries picked in nearby bogs.

suffered, but the railroad assured the continuation of the community and eventually it grew as it became a service and trade center for farmers and for the tourist industry.

Isle, the largest community on the lake today, was not "born" until 1913. In that year, a bank and several other business ventures appeared. Today, Isle serves the agriculture and tourist industries and is the location of a tackle manufacturing company and a metal plating operation - both now owned by the Ray-O-Vac Company. Nearly every major metal fishing lure manufactured in the Upper Midwest is plated at Isle.

As the forests disappeared, farming began in earnest and the deeply-rooted stumps were laboriously removed by axe, shovel, and grub hoe with the help of teams of horses or oxen. The fertility of the soil was spotty and dairying eventually proved to be the most economically productive enterprise in the lake area.

COMMERCIAL HUNTING AND FISHING

Once rail transportation was available to the Twin Cities markets, commercial fishing and hunting came to the lake. Although done mostly by Indians, many Whites were also involved. Not content with ordinary weapons, huge shotguns (up to 4 gauge) were mounted on the prows of launches and were loaded with everything from lead pellets to small fragments of scrap metal. These huge weapons were particularly devastating on the large rafts of bluebills, canvasbacks, and redheads that covered the lake during their migrations each spring and fall. Commercial hunting came to an end prior to World War I, but commercial fishing continued a short while after the war with the fish being sold in those last years through game wardens. The seining of rough fish - such as carp - continues to this day, but under the supervision of the Department of Natural Resources of the State of Minnesota.

Mille Lacs was not the only Minnesota lake harvested by commercial fishermen and hunters, but because of its nearness to markets was effected more than most. Lower Red Lake and Lake of the Woods are netted commercially to this day (1977) and Leech Lake is still netted for personal use by the Indians of that reservation area. During the late 1800's and the very early 1900's there were both commercial hunting and fishing operations on most large Minnesota lakes.

RESORTS AND RECREATION

With its excellent population of walleyes and its nearness to the Twin Cities, Mille Lacs was among early 20th century resort centers of our state. By 1915, fishing camps and boat liveries were already appearing on the lake, particularly along the south shore. In 1925, tourist booklets and other promotional materials listed such names as Bay View, Izatys, Cozy Cover, Murray Beach, Rocky Reef, Shore Acres, Lakeside Inn, and the Blue Goose Resort - all of which are still in operation.[1]

Launches appeared in the decade before World War I, but were initially used more for sightseeing or even hauling freight rather than fishing. Since outboard motors were relatively scarce - even as late as the 1930's - most fishing was done from row boats and necessarily close to shore. Walleye fishing reached a peak shortly after Memorial Day (Decoration Day in those days) and was all through by the Fourth of July. However, once launches discovered summer walleyes well out in the lake, resorters began towing row boats out each morning and picking them up late in the afternoon. Mille Lacs Lake has long been known for storms that come up with little warning and a tranquil sheet of water can be turned into a churning sea in a matter of minutes. If launches were not quick to respond to storm warnings, a very dangerous situation would result. Over the years a good many drownings occurred.

[1]Fellegg, Joe, Jr., Mille Lacs Walleye Capital: 50 years ago, "Fins and Feathers", December Issue, 1974.

The first "luxury" hotel on Mille Lacs Lake—contructed in 1885 by T. E. Potts.

In these early years, most fishermen used cane (bamboo) poles and dozens were stacked in racks at nearly every resort. Some even used droplines. When the first "rods and reels" made their appearance, the level wind or "anti-backlash" device - as it was first called - had not yet been invented. In the early years, minnows were used - almost exclusively - as bait. The June Bug Spinner received early recognition on the lake and this was followed by the Prescott spinner. Following World War II, artificial lures rose in prominence, but today, live bait is once again the most popular, with leeches and nightcrawlers being used as much as - or even more - than minnows.

Veteran fishermen of the lake say that walleyes are actually running larger today than in "the good old days." Whether this was caused by commercial fishing or the absence of a stocking program in that day or for some other reason - we don't know. But fishing was excellent in those early years and many limits were even caught from shore each spring.

Few lakes have had the fishing pressure of Mille Lacs. Even in winter, from five to seven thousand fish houses make their appearance each year. Yet, fishing continues excellent for walleyes and lunker-size northerns. The Department of Natural Resources lists other varieties of fish found in the lake as yellow perch, rock bass, bluegill, pumpkinseed, largemouth bass, tullibees, black-brown and yellow bullhead, dogfish, white sucker, burbot, carp, and troutperch.

There is probably no better example of what good fish management can do to produce millions of hours of pleasure and recreation each year for thousands of fishermen. And if a list were to be compiled of the best walleye water in our country - Mille Lacs Lake would have to be at, or very near, the top of that list.

Fishing boats lining up to be towed far out on the lake for mid-summer fishing. Cane (Bamboo) poles were the favorite tackle. Nearly every resort had large racks of poles ready for purchase or rent.

Late winter tullibee fishing can be great. Jack Giza shows how it's done.

Even in the "good old days" Mille Lacs didn't produce walleyes like this! These young "night fighters" are (left to right) Paula Dravis, Pam Mergens, Blaine Dravis, Greg Dravis, Earl Mergens, Jeff Dravis.

CHAPTER SIX
The Red Lakes

Lower Red Lake, with its 180,868 acres of water and 69 mile shoreline, is the largest body of water entirely within Minnesota's borders.

Upper Red Lake, with 107,832 acres and 58 miles of shoreline, is fourth largest, exceeded in size only by Mille Lacs Lake and Leech Lake.

Together, they represent the southern remnant of Lake Agassiz - the great inland sea that was formed by the melting of the Pleistocene Glacier. Once larger than the Great Lakes, it remains are still awesome, and in addition to the Red Lakes include Lake of the Woods, Lake Winnipeg, Lake Manitoba, and scores of smaller bodies of water.

Several thousands of years ago, as the glacier receded, vegetation sprang up in its place. Animal life soon repossessed the land including the woolly mammoth, giant bison, caribou and elk - as well as the wild life we now associate with the Red Lake area.

Shortly thereafter came the Indians: the Laurel Culture, the Blackduck Culture, and then - probably in the 1600's - came the Sioux.

Although we know little about the years when the Dakotas (Sioux) inhabited the shores of the Red Lakes, the journal of Pierre La Vérendrye, builder and first commandant of Fort St. Charles on Lake of the Woods, describes a Cree-Monsonis raid in 1734 on Sioux villages, which most historians believe were located on the Red Lakes. The raid was in reprisal for the killing of four Cree Indians by the Sioux. The action was particularly significant in that it foretold the end to the truce negotiated by Du Luth some fifty-five years earlier between the Sioux and the Ojibway - Cree - Assiniboines Alliance.

Shortly after Christmas, 1733, La Vérendrye was summoned by his French colleagues to Fort St. Pierre on Rainy Lake, to try to persuade the Indians to keep that peace. The French knew there would be little time for the Indians to trap and hunt if they were at war with each other. After a grueling nine day journey on foot, La Vérendrye began his council with the Indians. In spite of his best efforts, they did not agree to abandon their plan for attack, but were willing to postpone any such action until spring - providing La Vérendrye would be willing to send his eldest son, Jean Baptiste, on the raid with them. He accepted this stipulation with great reluctance and in the hope tempers would cool with the passing of winter and the peace would be continued. But in the spring, a small army of 700 braves - mostly Cree - showed up at Fort St. Charles, fully expecting young La Vérendrye to join them. Heartsick with anxiety, the father wrote in his journal:

"How can I place my eldest son in the hands of these barbarians? Who knows that my son will ever return or that he will not be made prisoner by the Mascoutans Paunes, the sworn enemies of the Crees and Monsonis, who want me to let him go. On the other hand, if I refuse to let him go, I have reason to fear they will charge me with cowardice and come to the conclusion that the Frenchmen are cowards."

But La Vérendrye did keep his word and Jean Baptiste joined the huge war party - probably bound for the villages on Red Lake. The raid was apparently successful, and Jean Baptiste returned safely to his worried father - only to die two years later on June 5, 1736, in the famous Lake of the Woods massacre - when the Dakotas expressed their displeasure over the Frenchmen's friendship and support for their enemies by killing young La Verendrye, Father Alneau, and nineteen French soldiers and voyageurs. The party was on its way back east to see what had happened to their over-due winter supplies and had left the fort (just that afternoon) in order to reduce the number who would have to winter there.

Although La Verendrye did not yield to pressure from the Crees, Monsonis, and Ojibways to attack the Sioux in reprisal, the Indians themselves used it as an excuse to punish them. Far to the south, in La Pointe (on Lake Superior) an Ojibway war party set out to raid Sioux villages in southern Minnesota - using the Lake of the Woods incidents as an excuse. And thus the Cree and Monsonis raid on the Red Lake villages of the Sioux in 1734, helped destroy the peace negotiated by Du Luth on the shores of Lake Superior in 1678. The story is also a good illustration of the historical interdependence of the larger Minnesota lakes and of the people who lived on their shores.

As war broke out in the later 1730's between the Dakotas and the Ojibway and their allies, the Red Lake villages of the Sioux were probably the most vulnerable - because of their location so close to the power base of the Crees, Assiniboines, Monsonis, and Ojibway on the lakes of the border country. By 1740, the Sioux had lost control of the Red Lakes, but this did not mean the invaders from the north automatically moved into the abandoned village sites. Sioux war parties seriously contended for control of northern Minnesota up to 1770 and war parties continued to raid the area almost up to the Sioux Uprising of 1862. But for the Sioux, it was a history of defeat after defeat including major battles at Sandy Lake about 1746, Cut-Foot Sioux in 1748, the Mouth of the Sandy River in 1765, and Leech Lake in 1766. In the 1765 action, the Ponemah Indians of Red Lake completely annihilated an entire Sioux war party. Thereafter, the Sioux pretty much abandoned the Red Lake area - but there were other encounters such as the Battle of Chief's Mountain in 1796 (west of Red Lake) and the Battle of Thief River sometime between 1810 and 1815.

The year 1792 is usually accepted as the date the Ojibway settled permanently on the Red Lakes - nearly ten years after Sandy Lake and Leech Lake had become important Chippewa centers. The early Ojibway settlers on Red Lake were a part of the hunting and trapping contingent organized by Jean B. Cadotte, the French explorer about whom we read in our "Tales of the Crow Wing." Some settlers came from the border country - about sixty from Rainy Lake in one group and still others came from the Sandy and Leech Lake areas.

Close relationships existed among the Ojibway tribes of all the lakes of northern Minnesota and southern Ontario and the trails between them were well worn by Indian moccasins. Frequent mention of the Red Lake villages is made in the history and traditions of the other major lakes. Because marriages within each totem (or relation) were taboo, there was much inter-marriage among the communities of the different lakes. Also, families from the villages of various lakes often traveled together to winter hunting grounds. The Red Lake Indians, however, usually went west to hunt buffalo rather than to Long Prairie or up the Crow Wing River. Also, the larger war parties were frequently made up of braves from several villages. Although Red Lake warriors often joined with those of Leech, Cass, Winnibigoshish, and Sandy Lakes in raids to the south - their main responsibility was to protect against Sioux attacks from the west.

Chief Flat Mouth of Leech Lake told how he, as a young man, on one of his visits to the Red Lakes had joined in a raid to the western plains-in reprisal for the loss of some

Red Lake braves during an ill-fated fight with the Sioux way down at Battle Lake - a raid which had actually originated with the Leech Lake Ojibway. In spite of the travel limitations of that day, Minnesota's northwoods Indians did not live in isolated villages, but traveled extensively and often well beyond our state's borders as outlined today.

Another indication of the inter-mingling of the tribes is in the great number of Ojibway totems represented among the villages of Red Lake, including:

Bald Eagle	Lynx
Bear	Marten
Catfish	Mermaid
Crane	Moose
Eagle	Snake
Eelpout	Sturgeon
Elk	Wolf
Loon	Woodpecker
Rabbit	

Yet, there were differences in culture among the villages of the different lakes. For example, some archeologists hold that much of the pottery from Leech Lake was kiln dried - or at least fired in some way, while the Red Lake pottery was softer and probably sun-baked.

Early explorers of the region frequently encountered Red Lake Indians while visiting other lakes. A Red Lake Chief known as "Old Sweet" was on hand when Zebulon Pike visited Leech Lake in 1806, and his stirring speech in response to the Lieutenant's appeal for peace with the Dakotas is recorded on page 35.

WHITE EXPLORERS AND TRADERS

Both the Northwest Company and the American Fur Company had posts on the Red Lakes. No doubt over the years there were a number of traders who moved in to establish "winter posts" of relatively short duration, but more permanent operations were established by the North West Company on the east end of Red Lake (as indicated on a map drawn in 1806) and the American Fur Company (at Red Lake).

The Red Lakes have historically been more free of white man's influence than any of the major lakes of our state. This statement even holds true today. Because of where they are located and because of the difficult terrain both to the north and the south, the lakes were not easily accessible to either the French-Canadian explorers of the border lakes or those who approached what is now Minnesota via Lake Superior or the Mississippi River. Young Jean Baptiste La Verendrye could very well have been the first white man to see the Red Lakes (in 1734). We know that Jean Cadotte was there in 1792 and other traders probably visited the Red Lakes in the interim. An employee of the North West Company, David Thompson, encountered the Red Lakes in 1798 while on a mission to locate the 49th parallel and survey a route to the source of the Mississippi; he incorrectly identified Turtle Lake as the headwaters. The flamboyant Italian explorer, Count Giacomo Beltrami, traveled south from Pembina to the Red Lakes in 1823. Here he hired a guide to replace the two guides and an interpreter who had deserted him when they encountered a handful of Sioux warriors (actually the Sioux were probably leaving the area). Beltrami left Lower Red Lake by way of Mud Creek. Traveling south, he found a small, heart-shaped lake he named "Julia" and claimed it to be the source of both the Mississippi and the Red River of the north (and he was wrong twice).

MISSIONARY EFFORTS

The Red Lakes have long been a target area for missionaries. Credit for establishing the first mission - in 1842 - goes to Rev. Frederick Ayer. Previously, at the invitation of traders of the American Fur company, Ayer had started missions and schools at La Pointe (1830-31), Madeline Island (1832), Sandy Lake (1833), and Pokegama Lake (1836).

Originally Ayer had been sponsored by the American Board of Missions, but when he proposed to establish his work at Red Lake and Leech Lake with people associated with Oberlin College of Ohio, they withdrew their support - largely because they objected to the school's theology, which taught that a person could perfect himself and reach sanctification before death. Undaunted, Ayer and his recruits persisted and both missions were established. David Spencer was left in charge of the Red Lake Mission; he was replaced after a short stay by a Mr. Bernard who in turn was succeeded by Rev. Sela G. Wright. The Leech Lake post lasted only three years but the Red Lake Mission continued until 1857 when the missionaries finally wore out - from fighting the wilderness, the weather, liquor problems of the Indians, and apathy on the part of the natives. Other outposts were established for fairly brief periods of time on Cass, Winnibigoshish, and other lakes in the area. The work of the Oberlin group continued in the region until 1859.

An article on the Oberlin band of missionaries by William Bigglestone in the Spring 1976 Issue of "Minnesota History" gives us great insight into hardships endured by the early missionaries - and others - while traveling across the wilderness. Bigglestone quotes the "Oberlin Evangelist" of May 10, 1843, as follows:

It was deep into the winter of 1842-43 when three men slowly worked their way through the frozen swamps and forests to the west and northwest of Lake Superior. They followed Indian trails and each evening at sundown stopped to make camp. Logs 8 to 10 feet in length were cut to feed an all-night fire, and balsam fir branches were gathered for the foundation of a bed. After the snow had been cleared away with a snowshoe there was room for a fire, a bed, two dogs and the loaded sled that the dogs pulled. When twigs or dry grass had been laid atop the branches of the bed, the three put on dry leggings and moccasins, ate supper, sany a hymn, and united in prayer. They they lay down together on the one bed, sometimes wearing caps, coats, and mittens because they had not room to carry sufficient bedding for the extreme cold. If the wind blew too fiercely they put up a row of branches to break its force and hoped the fire would not have to be renewed often during the night. They arose before daylight for a breakfast of rice or boiled corn meal thickened with flour and sweetened by a little sugar, and, while preparing it, they also baked bread cakes which served as a noon meal that could be eaten while walking.

The three men described were Frederick Ayer, David Spencer, and a young Ojibway guide named Yellow Bird; their destination was Red Lake. Bigglestone also tells of a summer journey from Oberlin College to Red Lake by a party headed by S.T. Bardwell and which included three men, three women and some children:

Among the obstacles they faced were cholera and other illness; flooding rivers; mosquitoes so thick they were almost inhaled when one drew breath; straying horses; portages with mud and water higher than boot tops; flies so thick their bites left a child's hair matted in her blood under her bonnet and her ear filled with clotted blood;

high winds that almost swamped canoes as they crossed lakes; and summer heat that rose to a temperature of a hundred degrees.[1]

In 1851, Bardwell reported concerning the work of the Oberlin Mission at Red Lake: "Here a school was taught nine months with twenty-one scholars, with an average attendance of nine. Four have been boarded and clothed entirely by the mission. Many of the children enter the school in a state of nudity, and we are obliged to furnish them clothing." A discouraging picture? Not at all relatively speaking. Bardwell went on to say, "Red Lake prospects are more encouraging than those at either Cass Lake or Winnibigoshish stations. They will raise the present season an abundant supply of corn and potatoes. They are becoming more industrious and making more rapid improvement than any other band in the territory. They are beginning to feel in some measure the importance of educating their children."

A Catholic Mission was opened at Red Lake in 1858 by Father Lawrence Lautischar who came to the Red Lakes from Crow Wing on August 15th of that year. He shared a house with a trader named Joseph Jourdain - located just to the east of the agency building. Although his work in opening the mission was significant, his labors were cut short by his untimely death on December 3. Father Lautischar froze to death while crossing the lake! It is believed he was returning from a visit to the Cross Lake Indians (Ponemah). Following his death, the mission was continued as an outreach of the Crow Wing church with visitations by Fathers Francis Pierz (1858-1867) and Joseph Buh (1867-75). Father Tomazin of White Earth visited the mission from 1875 to 1879 and in that year moved to Red Lake permanently where he served until 1883. Father Aloysius Hermanutz took over the work in 1883 and continued to 1888; however, he was headquartered during this time at White Earth. In 1888, Fathers Thomas Borgerding and Simon Lampe arrived from St. John's Abbey and established St. Mary's Mission at its present site.

In 1875, Rev. Francis Spees established a work on the lakes under the sponsorship of the American Missionary Association.

Two years later, in 1877, the Episcopal Mission was founded by Rev. Samuel Madison, Rev. Fred Smith, and Rev. J.A. Gilfillan. The men appropriated an abandoned log cabin at Red Lake which served as both home and chapel. in 1880 a new log church was constructed. Rev. Smith served the parish for eleven years and was succeeded by a number of Indian missionaries. In 1878, the Episcopal missionaries attempted to establish a mission at Ponemah, but it met with considerable resistance. At that time the village was called "Cross Lake" or "O-bash-ing." Most of the missionaries at Red Lake considered these people as the most difficult to deal with and openly referred to them as "pagans." Actually, the village was as isolated from white influence as any in the country at that time.[2] Following this frustrating experience, the Episcopalians turned to Ondatamaning or "Old Chief's Village" - now called Redby - and established a new mission there in December 1878. In 1896, the "Sybil Carter Indian Mission and Lace Industry Association" - an outreach of the Episcopal Church - established their program at Red Lake with Miss Sophy Styles as teacher. Twelve of these little industries were started in the country; three of them in Minnesota: Red Lake, Leech Lake, and White Earth.

Although the work of the missionaries at the Red Lakes and elsewhere in Minnesota was intended to be helpful to the Indians and in no way should be "put down," their

[1]Bigglestone, William, "Oberlin College and the Beginning of the Red Lake Mission. **Minnesota History,** Spring issue, 1976.

[2]The first mission was established in Ponemah in 1928.

efforts in teaching the principles of Christianity must have been quite confusing to the native Americans. Not only was it a new and foreign religion, but each denomination had a little different approach. The fact that all Whites did not accept or abide by the teachings of the churches, did not help the credibility of the missionaries. No wonder that many Indians kept their ancestral religious beliefs or melded their own traditions with Christian teachings. But many Indians were "converted" and in turn became effective missionaries to their own people.

EDUCATION

The education of the Indian children of the Red Lakes reflects the constantly changing attitude of the federal government towards our native Americans. Initially, everyone was content to leave education in the reservation areas in the hands of the missionaries, and we have seen how both the Protestant and Catholic missions at Red Lake responded with boarding schools for the Indian children. The very first mission - established by Frederick Ayer had a school in operation by 1843 or 1844. Two Catholic Sisters arrived in 1888 (the same year Fathers Borgerding and Lampe took charge of the Red Lake Mission) and started a small boarding school in the old American Fur Company store building.

Alexander Ramsey in 1852 - while Territorial Governor - issued an order abolishing religious schools on reservations and attempted to create "manual-labor schools" in their place. These forerunners to vocational schools were actually established but in many cases were finally given to the missionaries to operate. Thus, the same teachers continued on in many cases, but were usually reluctant to accept the new philosophy of education. D.B. Herriman, who was an Ojibway Indian Agent for the area including Red Lake in 1853, argued for the manual-labor (or manual training) concept; in his report of that year he urged, "that the boys be taught the use of tools and be put in various shops to learn anything useful; that the teachers allow no Indian dress to be made in the school nor worn by the scholars; that they learn to wash, bake, knit, make soap and candles, to reside in houses, sleep in beds, eat at tables on plates, with knives and forks; and in general that their culture be changed. Let books be a secondary consideration, except to those who are too young to handle tools." But in the end, the vocational philosophy was compromised and the "literacy school" concept was somewhat reinstated.

In 1877, a government boarding school was established at Red Lake with a capacity of fifty students. Later, a day school was added (actually a separate building) and in 1885 there were fifty students in the boarding school and twenty students lived at home and walked to school daily. In the 1890's the manual-labor schools were replaced across the country by government "contract schools" and the Red Lake boarding school was enlarged under the new program (1896). In 1900, the government constructed a new boarding school at Red Lake with a capacity for 100 students and nearly all of the materials were hauled across country from Solway by "tote team." An attempt was also made in the same year to build a boarding school at Cross Lake (Ponemah), but the Indians did not want their burial grounds disturbed or any of their homes affected and they threatened to burn down any school the government might build. Eventually a compromise was worked out and the school was built east of the narrows; it opened in January of 1901. The school soon had an enrollment of sixty students, about two-thirds of which were boarded. By 1905, the

St. Mary's Boarding School had been expanded to serve eighty students. As a "contract school," St. Mary's was eligible for federal support.

In 1907 the U.S. Commissioner for Indian Affairs (Leupp) declared that all boarding schools on reservations were "alien to the spirit of American life" and recommended that they be replaced by "day schools." Under this new policy, an elementary school was constructed at Redby, which opened in 1888. In 1912, a public school was organized at Red Lake in one of the rooms of the government boarding school and was given the designation as "Unorganized District No. 119" by the Minnesota State Department of Education. The public school system grew to replace the government school and a Superintendent of Schools was hired. Meanwhile the Redby school was replaced with a structure housing three classrooms and a library (1924), and this, too, was placed under the jurisdiction of the Superintendent of Schools at Red Lake in 1936.

Today, the Red Lake Schools are operated as public schools, with their own school board, as District No. 38, State of Minnesota. In addition to state aids they receive "Johnson-O'Malley"[1] funds and other aids from the Bureau of Indian Affairs in Washington, but as a closed reservation the people are in control of their own schools.

AGRICULTURE

When white men first arrived at Red Lake they found the Ojibway there were a-mong the best farmers of any of the Indian people in the entire midwest. In the winter of 1842-43 they had enough grain and vegetables to feed about fifty families from other bands who came there to escape starvation. Following the harvest in 1843, the agent at La Pointe, Wisconsin, (Alfred Brunson) purchased over $100 worth of surplus corn from the Red Lake Indians, which he distributed to other bands. In 1866, the agent in charge of the area reported that he had eight government oxen stationed at Red Lake and that "at least 130 acres were plowed." The 1868 grain crop amounted to over 7000 bushels. Subsequent reports by agents indicate that the Red Lake Indians seemed to always have enough food, even while other tribes experienced drought or plagues of grasshoppers.

LOGGING OPERATIONS

The Nelson Act of 1889 authorized Indians to cut "dead and down timber" on their own lands. However, these kinds of logs brought only 50 cents per thousand feet compared to the going rate of $3/thousand for Norway and $3.50/thousand for White Pine. It was the first opportunity for the Ojibway to receive money for anything except furs or the few dollars they had received for surplus crops. It has been said that there seemed to be just enough fires in those days to make sure the supply of dead timber never ran out. Folwell, in his "History of Minnesota,"[2] reported eleven million feet were cut on reservation lands by 300 Indians aided by eight Whites during the winter of 1889-90. In later years it became possible for Whites to bid on standing timber on Indian lands: however, judging by the prices, there is little doubt there was collusion.

Lumbering remains the principal source of income for the reservation. In 1924 a large new mill was constructed at Redby; since that time the Red Lake Indian Mills have provided the major source of employment and income for the people living at

[1]"Johnson-O'Malley" is the name of the federal legislation which provides special aids to any school which has over a minimum percentage of Indian children enrolled.

[2]Folwell, William Watts, a 'History of Minnesota,' Minnesota Historical Society, 1956.

the south end of Lower Red Lake. Actually, the first sawmill was at Red Lake. Bardwell reported in 1856, "We have erected a good water mill for sawing lumber, with a portable grist mill attached." In 1868, a sawmill and grist mill were erected near the mouth of Mud Creek. In 1907, a sawmill which had been constructed at Shell Lake in 1892 (seven miles from Red Lake), was moved to Red Lake.

Adolph Lundy in his booklet about his Red Lake boyhood tells of his memories of log drives on the Clearwater River at the turn of the century.

"When the logs were running in the river, especially at night when everything was quiet, we could hear the logs bumping against each other. It was an interesting sound, almost like music. It was like someone pounding on a bass drum. It would be two bumps close together and then after awhile two more or one single and so on. A person could lay and listen to it until he went to sleep. It was so interesting and you could hear it for a mile or more. In the daytime, if the logs were running in the river, the drivers had it easy. They could just sit on a stump or log and watch the logs go by. But when they jammed up they had to get busy and try to get the logs moving again. It was a dangerous job! Sometimes they had to get out on the logs and pry the logs loose. When they got the right log loose, they would start to move and if there was alot of pressure behind them, they would sometimes come tumbling end over end down stream." [1]

EARLY TRANSPORTATION

Because of their remote location, the Red Lakes have always had transportation problems. As the first Whites came to the area, the historic travel routes of the Indians were used: from Detroit (now Detroit Lakes) and White Earth to the southwest, from the west by the Red Lake River, and from the Leech Lake and Cass Lake areas to the south. Huge swamps made the approach from the north and east very difficult. The first mail to Red Lake was carried on the backs of Indians from White Earth. Most freight came in winter when lakes, streams, and swamps were frozen. The freight route usually followed was from Detroit (now Detroit Lakes) via White Earth and, later, Fosston (when the railroad reached that community). In 1874 a road was opened between White Earth and Red Lake.

Steamboats made their first appearance on the lakes in 1890, and they were in heavy use for about twenty years. Among them were the "Mudhen" and the "Chippewa" which were both destroyed by ice in a spring breakup.

Logging brought the railroad to Redby in 1905. The Minnesota - Red Lake, and Manitoba Railway Company was granted the right of way. By the end of that year, the Red Lakes had rail service to Bemidji.

WHITE SETTLERS

The opening of ceded lands in this area to homesteading in the 1890's brought hundreds of White settlers. In 1896, homesteaders were required to pay a $14.50 land office filing fee and $1.25 an acre for the 160 acre tract they were allowed to claim. Many complained that the cost was prohibitive - and indeed it was for some in that day. Most homesteaders failed to make it. Although there is some good soil in the area, much of it is not too productive. Also, growing seasons were short for the varieties that could be planted in those times and the farms were too far from the markets of the larger population centers.

Adolph Lundy, in his book, "When I was a Boy in the Wilderness of Northern

[1] Lundy, Adolph, "When I was a Boy in The Wilderness of Northern Minnesota."

Minnesota," tells of traveling with his family from Fosston to the area open for homesteading.

"Finally, my uncle came and we all got into the covered wagon and we went Northeast towards his homestead. There were no roads, only Indian trails through the woods that went zigzag between the trees, barely wide enough for the wagon to get through. They were so rough! I can remember when we got to Leon Post Office. The storekeeper had cut about an acre or so of brush in front of the store and left only the big trees. That was the first opening I could remember since we left Fosston. I remember we rested the horses awhile before we went further. When we came to my uncle's homestead, I recall there being a small hut about 12 feet square, built out of popple logs that were about 16 inches in diameter. It had a birch bark roof with sod on top and homemade wooden hinges on the door. Both families lived in that shack for 2 or 3 weeks until my dad found a place for us for the winter. He finally found a place 1 mile East, not far from the Clearwater River. The house was owned by two Norwegian brothers by the names of Ole and John Faden. They had a homestead shack 12 by 20 feet built out of logs and divided into two rooms. They were going back to where they had come from for the winter and wanted someone to stay in the shack while they were gone. They had a saw mill on the river bank 1/2 mile East of the shack. We got to stay there until late in the spring. We lived on rabbits that my dad snared there. The woods were full of them. I can remember 3 or 4 rabbits hanging outside the door most of the time. When mother wanted one, she would have to take it in, thaw it out, clean it, and then prepare it for the table.

Lundy also told of the abundance of partridges, prairie chicken, and deer and how this wild game, together with fish, constituted their meat diet.

As if cold winters, deep snow, mosquitoes and flies in summer, and all the other perils of wilderness living were not enough, a sudden storm could smash the early settlers' dreams in a matter of minutes; Lundy recalled,

In the spring of 1901, we moved from the homestead to Tom Sandland's because there was so much water on the meadows. It was just across the road from Uncle Christianson's. We intended to move back on the homestead before haying started, but on the 5th of July a storm came up suddenly. It was about 6 o'clock in the evening and on a Saturday. My Mother had all our clothes hanging on the foot of the bed ready to be changed into and supper was on the table. I was told to call Tom for supper. He was working in the barn. Tom and I started for the house and it started to blow so hard from the Southwest that we just barely made it back to the house. The door was on the West side and when we got inside we had to hold the door shut. The wind was so strong that we could feel the wall go in and out. Suddenly Tom ran over and opened the celler door. He told us all to get in the celler as fast as we could. As soon as we were all in the celler, we heard the roof blow off. The house was built of logs and we could hear as the wind took the logs off way down to the upstair's floor joists. The upstair's floor wasn't nailed on, so that blew off too. The house was scattered all over in the woods. The storm didn't last very long and when it was over we got to see what had happened. The woods were laying flat to the ground. Only a few hardwood trees were standing and they were leaning at a 45 degree angle. The roof was wrapped around a clump of basswood trees like a blanket.

But the hardy pioneers did not give up and today, Tom Sandland's son, Truman, and his family operate one of the state's largest wild rice spreads from the original homestead.

COMMERCIAL FISHING

The Red Lake Fisheries Association is headquartered at Redby and provides the second largest source of income for the band. As with the sawmill, it is a cooperative enterprise. Although the fisheries building was constructed in 1924 on authority of the Minnesota State Legislature, commercial fishing really had its beginning on the Red Lakes during World War I. Prior to that time, the Indians netted fish for their own personal needs, but there was virtually no market; a four to seven pound whitefish brought ten cents and walleyes over a foot long - five cents! But during the war, there was a genuine concern about food shortage and the Minnesota Safety Commissioner founded the fishery at Redby to procure food for our state's public institutions. For the first time, commercial fishing became worthwhile for the Red Lake Ojibway.

A NATION WITHIN A NATION

We have said earlier that one of the reasons the Red Lake Indians have remained more free from white man's influence than most is the remote location of the Lakes. There is another and more important reason, and that is the historic refusal of the Red Lake band to sell their land to the U.S. Government. All other Minnesota bands signed treaties in the 19th century ceding their lands to the government in return for what seemed at the time to be large monetary settlements and worthwhile assurances. In contrast, the Red Lake Ojibway chose to continue holding their land in common. One by one the Indian tribes had yielded to the pressure and promises of the U.S. Land Commissioners[1] until by 1889 the Red Lake band remained the only holdout. We know that every effort was made to pressure and tempt this last group to follow the example of the other tribes. Not only were they offered the same monetary and other considerations but were subjected to tremendous peer pressure from the other Indians who flaunted their new wealth - temporary though it would be - and actually scorned the Red Lake band for not taking advantage of the government offer. The commissioners themselves used every sales technique "in the book" but the Red Lake leadership held firm.

Nah-gaun-e-gwon-abe (Leading Feather) pointed out that in earlier concessions the white man had profited much and the Indian, little. Chief May-dway-gwa-no-nind (He That is Spoken To) is quoted by Charles Brill in his book about the Red Lake Band entitled, "Indian and Free," as pleading - "I am getting aged; I see that I shall be called upon by the Master of Life to deliver an account of myself . . . I must look to my grandchildren and my children's grandchildren; I must look after the benefit of all . . . This property under discussion, called Red Lake, is my property. These persons who you see before you are my children. They own this place the same as I own it. My friends, I ask that we reserve the whole of the lake as ours and that of our grandchildren hereafter." Later, he added, "We wish to guarantee to our posterity some security; that is why we demand the reservation we have outlined on that paper. It is not greediness that influences us. The tribe is growing year by year, and we think it is our duty to protect those who come after us. We know the character of our country here. There are only meadows in certain places; there are trees we would get our fuel from. All these things do not grow together, so the tract must be made large so as to

---

[1]The Minnesota Commission, as constituted in 1889, included Henry Rice of Minnesota, Bishop Martin Marty of North Dakota, and Joseph Whiting of Wisconsin. Consultants were Bishop Whipple and Archbishop Ireland.

Ojibway fisherman tending his nets on Lower Red Lake.   Courtesy of the Minneapolis Tribune.

combine all the things we want. We want the reservation we now select to last ourselves and our children forever."[1]

In the end, on July 6, 1889, a treaty was signed giving up considerable land[2] for the payment of $90,000 a year for fifty years plus interest on monies accumulated from the sale of the ceded lands - but the reservation remained in tact and generally sovereign.

[1]Brill, Charles, "Indian and Free," U of M Press, 1974.
[2]2,905,000 acres.

Chief May-dway-gwa-no-nind (He that is spoken to). His leadership helped make Red Lake a sovereign nation.

Courtesy of the Minnesota Historical Society

In 1902, 256,152 additional acres in Red Lake County were ceded to the government for $1,000,000. In 1904 this treaty was amended so that the land was placed on auction bringing a somewhat higher return to the tribe ($1,265,000). This left a reservation area of 805,722 acres or 1,259 square miles - an area about the size of the State of Rhode Island.

In 1918, the General Council of the Red Lake Band of Chippewa Indians was organized. Although Joseph Jourdain was elected the first president, it was Peter Graves who is usually given the credit for organizing the council and drafting the constitution which established the governance for the reservation. The constitution even provided for the reservation's own system of courts and law enforcement. Graves was elected treasurer and later secretary treasurer; he was probably the most influential person on the reservation for the next forty years - up to the time of his death in 1957.

In 1958, Roger Jourdain was successful in leading an historic movement to revise the 1918 constitution, providing for an elected council of five chiefs and making the government, in general, more democratic. Jourdain was elected chairman of the tribal council and has been subsequently elected chairman every four years since. The council is unique in that it provides the business control and leadership as well as political direction for the reservation.

And so Red Lake continues as a nation within a nation. It is a closed reservation and enjoys a great degree of sovereignty. Residents are born as both Minnesota and United States citizens and may vote in elections - but they are not subject to the normal tax structure. Theirs is truly a dual citizenship.

COMMUNITIES OF THE LAKE

Membership in the Red Lake Band includes about 6000.[1] Of this number, about 2000 live off the reservation - mostly in the Twin Cities. The balance live for the most part on Lower Red Lake in the communities of Red Lake, Redby, and Ponemah.

RED LAKE, the largest of the three villages, is located on the south shore of the lower lake. An Indian village for generations, a North West Company post was established here in the early 1800's; later, the American Fur Company built a post here. Missions and schools were established in the 1840's. Red Lake remains the educational center for the reservation and has been the site of its only high school since 1935. Red Lake is the location for a public elementary school and the historic St. Mary's Mission School; both also serve the children of Redby. The Red Lake Indian Hospital has been located here since 1914.

Red Lake is an old village. Physicians were assigned here by the Chippewa Agency as early as 1865 (Dr. V.P. Kennedy). Chief Moose Dung (later a merchant) lead a delegation of Red Lake Indians to Washington in 1864. A white man, W.R. Spears, opened a store in the community in 1879. Prior to that date, he had begun his trading enterprise by following the Red Lake Indians around when they dug snake root (also called Seneca Root).[2] In 1875 the first post office in Beltrami County was opened at Red Lake. By 1893, other stores were added and even some small hotels. Red Lake became the "jumping off place" for White settlers and homesteaders. There was no other source of supplies for many miles around. In those days, visitors to the present site of Bemidji would have found no white man's village, only a Chief by that name.

[1] At least one-fourth Red Lake Indian blood is required for membership
[2] Reputed to have medicinal value, including a remedy for snake bite.

Courtesy of the Minnesota Historical Society

Chief Bemidji—The Ojibway Indian for whom Bemidji, Minnesota was named. His name - Shag-now-ish-kung" - means "Lake through which a river flows." Many travelers, both white and Indian, visited him on the shores of the lake for which he was named.

"Bemidji" means "lake through which a river flows." Actually, Chief Bemidji was not a chief and his real name was Shag-now-ish-kung.

REDBY is located five miles east of Red Lake on Highway 1. Although smaller than Red Lake, it houses the important sawmill, fisheries building, and a fish hatchery which was constructed here in cooperation with the Minnesota Department of Natural Resources. It, too, is an old village and was known originally as "Ondatamaning" or "Old Chief's Village" (after Chief Madwaganonint). It was officially platted as a village in 1905 by the Minnesota - Red Lake, and Manitoba Railway Company - but had been a settlement for many years before that.

The third village on Lower Red Lake is PONEMAH (which means "hereafter") originally called "Cross Lake" because of its location across the lake from Red Lake and Redby. It is one of the oldest continuously inhabited village sites in Minnesota and has always been one of the most isolated. It has its own elementary school but the high school students are transported to Red Lake. Five miles west of the village is Ponemah Point; it is also called the Narrows or "O-bash-ing" which means "a straight place where wind blows through." This area provides some of the best fishing grounds of the Reservation.

UPPER RED LAKE

We have said little about Upper Red Lake itself. This is because it has always been sparsely settled by either Indians or Whites. John Morrison, Jr., an early business leader at Red Lake and postmaster at Ponemah, told historian Charles Vandersluis that there were very few Whites on the upper lake at the turn of the century: Frank Lyon at Waskish (named for an Indian, Wahwanshkayslie - which means deer), Chris Rogers at Shotley Brook, and Albert Smith across the lake (from Shotley Brook). Today there are relatively few resorts on the lake even though fishing is excellent. The walleyes are uniformly small, averaging about one pound; yet, the northerns are large. Being relatively shallow, the Red Lakes are really natural rearing ponds. Commercial fishing operations on the lower lake are usually blamed for the small size of the walleyes, but other theories also abound.

The remainder of the fish population is interesting in that it includes the sheepshead and the goldeye - both relatively uncommon in Minnesota lakes. There are remarkably few other varieties; The Department of Natural Resources lists whitefish, yellow perch, and white sucker as the only other species.

Because woodland caribou once inhabited the area, a herd was reintroduced after World War I north of the lakes; unfortunately, they were quickly wiped out by poachers.

Upper Red Lake, with its excellent fishing and hunting and vast wilderness area, is our state's largest, under-used, water-based, natural resource.

No hunting or fishing by Whites is permitted on the reservation surrounding Lower Red Lake - except as guests of the band. Although hunted heavily, the area supports large herds of deer and moose as well as an abundance of smaller game and fur bearing animals. Fishing in all the lakes is excellent. The reservation may be the largest concentration of wildlife in our state.

And from where comes the name "Red" lakes? Anyone who has watched the water churning on a windy day knows the answer to that question. The color, of course, comes from the soil on the lake bottom. "Old timers" insist, however, that both lakes were once more red than today.

Chris & Chad Longbella display three limits of Red Lake Walleyes. Although not large, they are an ideal size for eating. Red Lake is probably the most dependable walleye water in Minnesota.

TREATIES BETWEEN MINNESOTA INDIAN TRIBES
AND THE UNITED STATES GOVERNMENT[1]

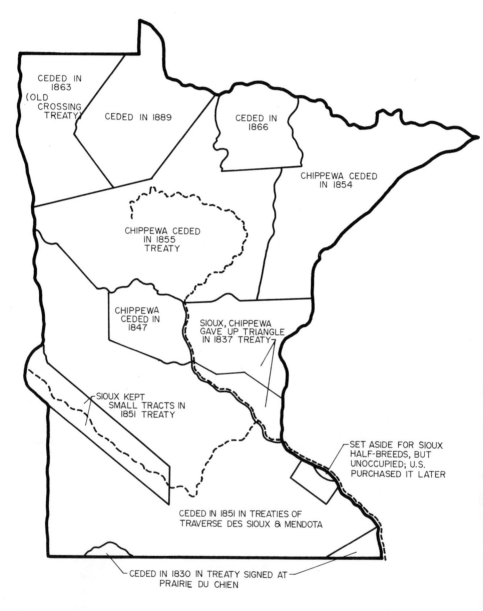

NOTES

old fe, p' so. !!!

Maya Rose
103 Great Plains Drive
Hills, MN
12-31-89

South West State
Bank
Hills, MN

Other Books by Duane R. Lund

A Beginner's Guide to Hunting and Trapping
A Kid's Guidebook to Fishing Secrets
Fishing and Hunting Stories from The Lake of the Woods
Andrew, Youngest Lumberjack
The Youngest Voyageur
White Indian Boy
Gull Lake, Yeaterday and Today
Lake of the Woods, Yesterday and Today, Vol. 1
Lake of the Woods, Earliest Accounts, Vol. 2
Lake of the Woods (The Last 50 Years and the Next)
Leech Lake, Yesterday and Today
The North Shore of Lake Superior, Yesterday and Today
Our Historic Boundary Waters
Our Historic Upper Mississippi
Tales of Four Lakes and a River
The Indian Wars
101 Favorite Freshwater Fish Recipes
101 Favorite Wild Rice Recipes
101 Favorite Mushroom Recipes
150 Ways to Enjoy Potatoes
Camp Cooking, Made Easy and Fun
Cooking Minnesotan, yoo-betcha!
Early Native American Recipes and Remedies
Entertainment Helpers, Quick and Easy
Gourmet Freshwater Fish Recipes
Nature's Bounty for Your Table
Sauces, Seasonings and Marinades for Fish and Wild Game
The Scandinavian Cookbook
The Soup Cookbook
Traditional Holiday Ethnic Recipes - collected all over the world
101 Ways to Add to Your Income
Now That You Have Found It (For the New Christian)
Lessons in Leadership, Mostly Learned the Hard Way

About the Author

- EDUCATOR (RETIRED, SUPERINTENDENT OF SCHOOLS, STAPLES, MINNESOTA);
- HISTORIAN (PAST MEMBER OF EXECUTIVE BOARD, MINNESOTA HISTORICAL SOCIETY); Past Member of BWCA and National Wilderness Trails Advisory Committees;
- SENIOR CONSULTANT to the Blandin Foundation
- WILDLIFE ARTIST, OUTDOORSMAN.